T0065502

WORDS OF ENCOURAGEMENT WHILE AWAITING THE LORD'S RETURN

COMMENTS ON 1 AND 2 THESSALONIANS

E. RICHARD PIGEON, Ph.D.

WESTBOW
PRESS®
A DIVISION OF THOMAS NELSON
& ZONDERVAN

WestBow Press books may be ordered through booksellers or by contacting:

WestBow Press
A Division of Thomas Nelson & Zondervan
1663 Liberty Drive
Bloomington, IN 47403
www.westbowpress.com
844-714-3454

Because of the dynamic nature of the Internet, any web addresses or links contained in this book may have changed since publication and may no longer be valid. The views expressed in this work are solely those of the author and do not necessarily reflect the views of the publisher, and the publisher hereby disclaims any responsibility for them.

Scripture quotations are from The ESV® Bible (The Holy Bible, English Standard Version®), copyright © 2001 by Crossway, a publishing ministry of Good News Publishers. Used by permission. All rights reserved.

ISBN: 978-1-6642-3479-6 (sc)
ISBN: 978-1-6642-3478-9 (e)

Print information available on the last page.

WestBow Press rev. date: 06/11/2021

CONTENTS

ABBREVIATIONS OF THE BOOKS OF THE NEW TESTAMENT

Matt.	:	Matthew
Mark	:	Mark
Luke	:	Luke
John	:	John
Act.	:	Acts
Rom.	:	Romans
1 Cor.	:	1 Corinthians
2 Cor.	:	2 Corinthians
Gal.	:	Galatians
Eph.	:	Ephesians
Phil.	:	Philippians
Col.	:	Colossians
1 Thes.	:	1 Thessalonians
2 Thes.	:	2 Thessalonians
1 Tim.	:	1 Timothy
2 Tim.	:	2 Timothy
Titus	:	Titus
Phm.	:	Philemon
Heb.	:	Hebrews

Jas.	:	James
1 Pet.	:	1 Peter
2 Pet.	:	2 Peter
1 John	:	1 John
2 John	:	2 John
3 John	:	3 John
Jude	:	Jude
Rev.	:	Revelation

PAUL'S FIRST LETTER TO THE THESSALONIANS

INTRODUCTION

Thessaloniki, also known as Thessalonica, is a city in northern Greece. Its municipality today has approximately 325,000 inhabitants, while the population of the metropolitan area is greater than 1,000,000. It is the second largest center in the country, after the capital Athens. King Cassander of Macedonia founded Thessaloniki in 315 BC. In the time of the apostle Paul, this city was the most populated in Macedonia and the capital of one of the four provinces of this region. Thessaloniki, along with Ephesus and Corinth, was actively involved in the maritime trade of the Aegean Sea.

The city of Thessaloniki was one of the locations providing a foothold for preaching the gospel in Europe and, as such, it is of particular interest to Christianity. We read in chapter 16 of the book of Acts how the Apostle Paul and his companions Silas and Timothy were prevented by the Holy Spirit on two occasions from preaching the Word of God in Asia. Following a night vision, they conclude that the Lord called them to evangelize those in Macedonia. So they set out for this destination.

Following their footsteps, we find that the city of Philippi is the first city they visited, in the year 49 AD, during Paul's second missionary journey. The gospel is preached; souls are saved and baptized in spite of Satan's opposition. Paul and Silas are promptly accused of disturbing the city and dragged before the rulers, where they are whipped and thrown into prison. In spite of these apparently adverse circumstances, the Word of the Lord is proclaimed to the jailer and his house with happy results. The city authorities meanwhile learn that those whom they have mistreated, without first judging them, are Romans. Realizing that they had just broken Roman laws, they beg Paul and his friends to leave the city.

From Philippi, Paul and Silas go to Thessalonica. This visit is recorded in Acts 17:1-9. There, Paul explains and proves during three Sabbaths that Christ had to suffer and rise from the dead. The result is remarkable: a few Jews, a multitude of Greeks, and a fairly large number of prominent women, persuaded by this preaching, join Paul and Silas.

Jewish jealousy, however, interrupts this work, so well begun. Paul and Silas are obliged to leave Thessalonica by night, sent by the brothers to Berea. There again, souls are won to Christ. Again, the Enemy is active, unable to bear such a testimony. Paul is sent off on his way by the brothers from Berea and is led to Athens. From there he goes to Corinth.

It is during this stay in Corinth, probably in the year 50 or 51 AD, that Paul writes this first letter to the believers in Thessalonica, whom he had left in a hurry and about whom he was worried. The apostle's heart, despite the distance, had remained with his dear Thessalonians. In chapter 2 of the letter, we learn that Paul wanted to visit them, but that Satan had prevented him from doing so; in chapter 3, he sent Timothy to strengthen and comfort them. Having received good news from Timothy about their faith, Paul himself is encouraged. This is the opportunity for him to write this letter, the first of all his letters preserved in the New Testament.

The purpose of Paul's first letter to the Thessalonians is to encourage these young believers and, of course, all those who would later read this letter. The word for encouragement (*paraklesis*) appears nine times in the original language. It is also translated "exhortation" and "consolation".

For ease in studying Paul's letter to the Thessalonians, its dominant theme, encouragement, suggests seven sections: Paul encouraged by the remembrance of those in Thessalonica (chap. 1); the Thessalonians encouraged by Paul's visit (chap. 2); Paul encouraged by the news brought by Timothy (chap. 3); the Thessalonians encouraged to walk in holiness (chap. 4:1-12), encouraged to wait for the Lord's coming for His people (chap. 4:13-18), encouraged to watch and to edify one another before the day of the Lord (chap. 5:1-11), and encouraged as brothers and sisters in the Lord by various exhortations (chap. 5:12-28).

The second coming of the Lord Jesus is certainly the encouragement par excellence that the Holy Spirit places before us in this letter. Whether for the saints or with the saints, the Lord's imminent return is the true Christian hope, our encouragement, and our consolation. Let us note the five mentions of the coming of the Lord and its effects: it delivers us from the wrath to come (1:10), it manifests the glory and the joy of the faithful servant (2:19, 20), it strengthens our hearts in holiness (3:13), it consoles us with regard to our deceased Christian brothers and sisters (4:13-18), and it urges us to keep ourselves blameless while waiting for the Lord's return (5:23).

The quotations from the New Testament are taken from the translation of the "English Standard Version" (2007). At the end of the book there is a glossary of the terms highlighted in the quoted verses, such as church, grace, peace. These definitions are taken from the author's Comprehensive Dictionary of New Testament Words, published in 2014.

May the Holy Spirit encourage us to persevere in reading Paul's first letter to the Thessalonians and the commentaries that accompany these verses: to persevere until the Lord's imminent return. He is coming soon! "Amen. Come, Lord Jesus!" (Rev. 22:20).

I

PAUL'S REMEMBRANCE OF
THE THESSALONIANS

Chapter 1

The first chapter of Paul's first letter to the Thessalonians highlights three important features of the Christian life: faith, love, and hope. Faith characterizes all those who believe in the Lord Jesus and His work on the cross. True faith is then manifested in those who are born again by visible fruit: the love of God, as well as the love of brothers and sisters in the Lord. Finally, the love of the Savior, the Lord Jesus, produces in those whom He has redeemed the expectation of His coming: this is the hope of His return to take them to be with Himself.

For the apostle Paul, the remembrance of these three precious features of the Thessalonians' Christian life was a subject of gratitude to God and of personal encouragement.

a. *Greetings (1:1)*

Paul, Silvanus, and Timothy, To the church of the Thessalonians in God the Father and the Lord Jesus Christ: Grace to you and peace. (1:1)

These greetings from three brothers to the church of the Thessalonians are both simple and warm. Paul does not mention his official title of apostle, as he does in most of his other letters. He associates with himself the two brothers who had worked with him in Thessalonica. Timothy, his true child in the faith as he called him, had returned to strengthen and encourage the Thessalonians. Silvanus, presumably known as Silas in the book of Acts, had also accompanied Paul during his first journey; it is very likely that he is the Silvanus whom Peter considers to be a "faithful brother" (1 Pet. 5:12).

All the Christians in Thessalonica at that time formed the church, or assembly, of that city. The local church is not strictly speaking a physical building. The term refers to a gathering of people who have believed in the Lord Jesus and have accepted His salvation. He has promised His presence to those who gather this way in His name (see Matt. 18:20).

The members of the church in Thessalonica already knew God revealed by the Lord Jesus in His most intimate relationship with the Father. "No one has ever seen God; the only God [or Son, in some manuscripts], who is at the Father's side, he has made him known" (John 1:18). The children of God know not only God, but the Father whom His Son has revealed to them. This is not a matter of intellectual understanding, but a personal relationship with divine persons. The appreciation and enjoyment of such a relationship are the privilege of the children of God through faith. In Paul's letters, only the church of Thessalonica is referred to as being in God the Father. This church is also seen as being in the Lord Jesus Christ, not only in the Savior. Already as a young church, it recognized the authority of the Lord and His rights over it, and over each of its individual brothers and sisters.

The actual greetings, "grace" and "peace", are the same in the salutations of all Paul's letters. In his individual letters to Timothy and Titus, the apostle adds "mercy", since it is more related to divine help for the individual. Grace can be defined as God's unmerited favor toward us: it is grace that "brings salvation for all people" (Titus 2:11), that "is sufficient" for us on the way (2 Cor. 12:9), and "that will be brought to you at the revelation of Jesus Christ" (1 Pet. 1:13). Peace encompasses both peace with God, when we have confessed our sins and turned to Him (Rom. 5:1), and the peace of God, which keeps our hearts and minds in Christ Jesus (Phil. 4:7). This first verse is, of course, about the peace of God rather than the peace with God.

b. *Reasons for thanksgiving (1:2-4)*

We give thanks to God always for all of you, constantly mentioning you in our prayers, (1:2)

The good news about the faith, love and hope of the Thessalonians, reported by Timothy, gives Paul the opportunity to make known his feelings towards the Christians of Thessalonica. It was not only for some brothers and sisters, who were perhaps closer than others to him, but for all, that he gave thanks. He did not do this only occasionally, but constantly or unceasingly.

What a beautiful lesson for us today! In moments spent in the presence of the Lord, we can speak to Him about our Christian brothers and sisters, and give thanks for them. We will always find a reason for which to thank Him for that brother or that sister, perhaps more distant or less kind, but for whom Christ gave His life and whom He loves. An obvious result of such a practice will be to strengthen the bonds of fraternal affection that unite us. Paul would later tell the Philippians that he gave thanks to his God for all the remembrance he had of them in *every* prayer of his for them all (Phil. 1:3, 4).

remembering before our God and Father your work of faith and labor of love and steadfastness of hope in our Lord Jesus Christ. (1:3)

Remembering his time with the Thessalonians, Paul has three subjects of gratitude to God: their faith, their love, and their hope; these three related virtues are indispensable to the Christian life. As has already been written, these three great principles were the powerful and divine motives for the life of the Thessalonians; they contributed to their joy (see v. 6). Their practical life flowed from their close relationship with God the Father and His Son, the Lord Jesus Christ. In Revelation 2, the church of Ephesus is said to have works, toil, and patient endurance. But it seems that, with the abandonment of its first love, for which the church is reproached, only an outward form remained. Ephesus had lost the fundamental Christian virtues of faith, love, and hope in the Lord Jesus.

The Christian faith replaces the law given by God to Israel, His earthly people. The works of the law cannot justify anyone, for by the law is the knowledge of sin. But by faith in the work of the Lord Jesus on the cross, we are justified freely by the grace of God. The work of faith is the outward manifestation of the faith implanted in us. Those who see our good works may give glory to our heavenly Father (Matt. 5:16). When we have put our trust in the person of the Lord and His work on the cross, we can walk in the good works that God has prepared in advance, i.e., practice those works (see Eph. 2:8-10).

Love, of course, is opposed to hatred. Before our conversion we were "hated by others and hating one another" (Titus 3:3). He who believes becomes a partaker of the divine nature and is able to love, for God is love (1 John 4:8). This love in our hearts is expressed in the work that results from it. It is not a work by obligation or of a mercenary, but a work of submission to and gratitude for the One who loved us and gave Himself for us (Gal. 2:20).

Concerning hope, Paul tells the Ephesians that we did not have hope in the past. We were then without Christ (Eph. 2. 12). Now Christ Jesus is our hope (1 Tim. 1:1). Since their conversion, the Thessalonians persevered in the patience of hope, i.e., the expectation of the return of the Lord Jesus Christ. The inner hope of the Christian is demonstrated in his patience: not in the restlessness of his thoughts and the feverishness of his continual actions, but in the calm assurance that the Lord is coming soon, as well as in serving Him intelligently and diligently.

Like those at Ephesus, some believers have only works, toil, and steadfastness, all of them visible to man. But, like those of Thessalonica, how much profitable it is to also possess the energy of faith, love, and hope. The resulting work, labor, and patience do not go unnoticed in the eyes of our God and Father.

For we know, brothers loved by God, that he has chosen you [literally: your election], (1:4)

Paul had quickly seen the fruit produced by the preaching of the gospel to the believers in Thessalonica. It is understandable that the term "brothers," used in the plural here and elsewhere in Paul's letter, refers to brothers and sisters since both men and women were active in the Church (see Acts 17:4). This was enough for him to recognize that God, in His eternal plans, had chosen these brothers and sisters even before the foundation of the world (see Eph. 1:4) and that He loved them. As for ourselves, believers in Christ, God has chosen us and loves us, too. Our acceptance of the gospel, i.e., the good news of God's salvation, confirms our election. Should not this encourage our souls, perhaps weary of the difficulties of the present life?

c. *Character of the gospel (1:5)*

because our gospel came to you not only in word, but also in power and in the Holy Spirit and with full conviction. You know what kind of men we proved to be among you for your sake. (1. 5)

This gospel preached by Paul and his companions, which had produced the work of faith, the labor of love, and the steadfastness of hope, was no ordinary message. The gospel, as we read, is the "power of God for salvation to everyone who believes" (Rom. 1:16). The English word "dynamism" is derived from the Greek word *dunamis* translated here as "power." The Holy Spirit, the divine person sent to the earth by the Lord, allows the power of the gospel to be manifested when it is preached. The result is understanding and assurance in the receptive listener, and even a full conviction, i.e., a great fullness of assurance, as in the case of the Thessalonians.

The spokesperson of the gospel, according to his or her personal relationship with God and His testimony, will facilitate or hinder the manifestation of the power of the Word of God, the free activity of the Holy Spirit and the assurance of those who listen. Paul's conduct had been beyond reproach, as the Thessalonians knew. It had not hindered the preaching of the gospel or its results.

The gospel is also distinguished by our love for souls. The Lord cannot use us effectively if we see in those who are not saved only their sins, their membership in a particular religious system, or their weaknesses. For example, we may know souls in a system resembling Sardis, having "the reputation of being alive, but (who) are dead" (Rev. 3:1), strangers to "the life that is in Christ Jesus" (2 Tim. 1:1). We may reject such a system, but we must not despise the souls in that system. Let us rather love souls to the extent that Christ loved us, for we too were in darkness before our conversion.

d. *Consequences of the gospel (1:6-8)*

And you became imitators of us and of the Lord, for you received the word in much affliction [or tribulation], with the joy of the Holy Spirit, (1:6)

It may seem surprising that Paul speaks of the Thessalonians as having become imitators of himself, firstly, and also, of the Lord. But this was not presumptuous. By imitating Paul, they became imitators of the Lord, for Paul followed the Lord. For to him to live was Christ

(Phil. 1:21). We are exhorted to consider the conduct of men like Paul and to imitate their faith (Heb. 13:7). Paul was a man with a nature similar to ours, to whom mercy was shown: he is an example for those who believe in the Lord Jesus for eternal life (1 Tim. 1:16). To imitate the Lord is to imitate Him who has all rights over us in the world that rejected Him and still rejects Him.

However, there is a price to pay when one wants to imitate the Lord, after having received the Word. "A disciple is not above his teacher, nor a servant above his master" (Matt. 10:24). Tribulations (other translations: trials, afflictions), such as opposition from those around us, often result from our commitment to the Lord at the beginning of the Christian life.

so that you became an example [or model, pattern] to all the believers in Macedonia and in Achaia. (1:7)

Verse 7 is a consequence of the previous verse. By preaching the Lord as a model and imitating Him, the Christian soon becomes himself a model for those who believe. It is not necessarily believers filled with spectacular gifts or manifesting great outward power who become role models for others. They are often brothers and sisters who suffer in silence for the name of the Lord, who persevere in spite of everything, but who are filled with the joy of the Holy Spirit. Let us also note that there had been no effort on the part of the Thessalonians to impose themselves as models. They had become models. Verse 8 tells us how.

For not only has the word of the Lord sounded forth from you in Macedonia and Achaia, but your faith in God has gone forth everywhere, so that we need not say anything. (1:8)

The power of the gospel, which is of God, had proved to be greater than the power of Satan. From the beginning, Satan had made every effort to interfere with Paul's work in Thessalonica and to discourage the young believers through great trials. But the word of the Lord continued to spread everywhere, supported by the eloquent testimony of the Thessalonians to God. Thessaloniki had a privileged geographical situation as a seaport where many people stopped and as a city crossed by one of the great roads of the Roman Empire, the Via Egnatia. The Christians of Thessaloniki therefore had the opportunity to proclaim the gospel to many visitors. Paul cannot help but notice this impressive manifestation of faith. What a powerful instrument the active faith of believers is for spreading the word of the Lord!

e. Testimony of the gospel (1:9, 10)

For they themselves report concerning us the kind of reception we had among you, and how you turned to God from idols to serve the living and true God, (1:9).

Not only did Paul have no need to say anything about the Thessalonians' faith in God, but he did not have to tell how the Holy Spirit had used him at the beginning in Thessalonica. This was well known in Macedonia and even further south in the region of Achaia. In addition, three things were reported about these new believers: their conversion, their service, and, in verse 10 which follows, their expectation.

Firstly, there were reports about the conversion of the Thessalonians. Their conversion had been an about-turn, a sudden change of direction. In the Greek original, we read that they had first turned to God away from idols. This presents us with an excellent explanation of what conversion is. God, first of all, draws us to Himself, which then leads us to leave idols. We must not believe that an idol is only a mute statue. It has been said that it is everything in the heart taking the place that belongs to God alone. In his or her new position, the one who has been converted can now "behold the glory of the Lord" (2 Cor. 3:18), thus enjoying His presence.

Secondly, the story of their service was reported. If the Thessalonians were converted, it was to serve the living and true God. What a contrast to serving lifeless and false idols! It must be recognized that God does not require the services of anyone of us. But in His grace, He offers us the privilege of being His servants in the fulfillment of His plans. Our responsibility as servants (the Greek word *doulos* also has the meaning of slave) is to set aside our own will and seek the Lord's will in order to do it. "I love my master," the Hebrew servant could say, "I will not go out free." Have we ever considered this for ourselves? "And he shall be his slave forever". What precious devotion! Let us remember that our Master was first the One who took the form of a servant, and that He became obedient to the point of dying on a Roman cross (see Exodus 21:2-6 and Phil. 2:5-11).

Thirdly, people were talking about the object of their expectation.

and to wait for his Son from heaven, whom he raised from the dead, Jesus who delivers us from the wrath to come. (1:10)

The Thessalonians were not occupied with the prospect of death or going to heaven, but with the coming of a resurrected Man, Jesus, from heaven. His tomb is empty. God has put His seal of approval on the work of His Son on the cross by resurrecting Him and making Him sit at His right hand in expectation of the day when He, the Son of Man, will return to judge the earth. But it is not as such that the Thessalonians expected Him or that we should expect Him. Jesus is coming to take us to be with Him and thereby save us from the wrath that will come upon an impious world that rejects God. For our encouragement, let us note that the Christian will not know these unparalleled judgments: "God has not destined us for wrath" (5:9), but "wrath has come upon them at last" (2:16). To reassure ourselves, we can also read Romans 8:1 and Revelation 3:10.

Our blessed hope (Titus 2:13) is the prospect of our great God and Savior Jesus Christ coming from heaven to take us to be with Himself at any time. How greatly this attitude of happy expectation manifested by the new converts at Thessalonica must have rejoiced Paul's heart and encouraged him in his own difficult circumstances! And as for ourselves, are we eagerly waiting for Him who is coming soon?

II

THE VISIT OF THE APOSTLE PAUL

Chapter 2

The apostle Paul, as we have just seen, was encouraged by the remembrance of the faith, love, and hope shown by the Thessalonians in his absence. We will now consider how the apostle, on his journey among them, had exhorted and consoled, and thus encouraged the Thessalonians to walk in a manner worthy of God. This second chapter of the epistle will also reveal Paul's feelings for those who had become dear to him.

a. *Welcoming the servants (2:1, 2)*

For you yourselves know, brothers, that our coming to you was not in vain. (2:1)

Verses 9 and 10 of the first chapter describe the results of Paul's coming to the believers in Thessalonica; the second chapter describes the character of Paul's work among them. To repeat an expression used by Paul elsewhere, "a wide door for effective work has opened to me" (1 Cor. 16:9). When God Himself opens the door, the work that follows is not in vain, but produces fruit to His glory. However, the verse in the Corinthians adds: "and there are many adversaries." We see this in the next verse.

14

But though we had already suffered and been shamefully treated at Philippi, as you know, we had boldness in our God to declare to you the gospel of God in the midst of much conflict. (2:2)

In Acts 16, we read that Paul and Silas had suffered at the hands of non-Jews in Philippi. After being flogged, they were thrown into prison and had their feet fastened in wooden stocks. In Acts 17, the opposition continued in Thessalonica, this time on the part of the jealous Jews. However, these perils did not diminish Paul's zeal to preach the gospel, for his boldness was not the result of his confidence in himself, but in his God.

The word *gospel* is found eight times in Paul's two letters to the Thessalonians. Five times he uses it in relation to God and the Lord Jesus Christ (1 Thess. 2:2, 8, 9; 3:2, 2 Thes. 1:8); three times Paul speaks of it in relation to himself (1 Thes. 1:5; 2:4; 2 Thes. 2:14). This expression "our gospel" in his letters is remarkable, and indicates the gospel faithfully proclaimed by Paul and his associates. Let us now look at what characterizes the gospel and the evangelist.

b. *Characteristic of the gospel preached (2:3-6)*

For our appeal [or encouragement, exhortation] does not spring from error or impurity or any attempt to deceive, (2:3)

We have in this verse the first mention of the word *paraklesis*, or encouragement, translated here as exhortation. By linking this verse with the previous one, we understand that the gospel is, so to speak, the first encouragement addressed to the lost sinner to come to Jesus. The purpose of the appeal of Paul and his colleagues was not to deceive or mislead; this would contradict the character of the living and true God (1:9). The gospel has a character of intrinsic purity; only man can alter it by adding to it or subtracting from it.

The gospel presented by Paul and his associates was not a trick, designed to deceive: their listeners did not have to fear some cleverly concealed trap. In this matter, those who seek dishonest pecuniary gain or undue prestige in evangelizing do not glorify God. Paul left us a model: in his preaching, he presented the gospel free of charge (1 Cor. 9:18). Of course, the Lord's worker deserves his wages (Luke 10:7; 1 Tim. 5:18).

Paul's exhortation was distinguished by its truth, purity, and sincerity. Therefore, God can approve such a gospel.

but just as we have been approved by God to be entrusted with the gospel, so we speak, not to please man, but to please God who tests our hearts. (2:4)

As with any Christian service, God's approval is necessary for one who begins in the service of the gospel. The Lord had said of Paul that he was "a chosen instrument of mine to carry my name before the Gentiles and kings and the children of Israel" (Acts 9:15). From the beginning of his ministry, we see Paul "proclaiming Jesus in the synagogues, saying that He is the Son of God" (Acts 9:20). God who has approved His servants tests their hearts. This testing is necessary for two reasons: so that no fault may be found in the servants' God-given ministry and so that no one will blame the Lord's servants (2 Cor. 6:3; 8:20).

It is true that not all of us are called to be evangelists, but we are encouraged to do "the work of an evangelist" (2 Tim. 4:5). We may, according to our own abilities, perform a service similar to that of the one who has received the gift of evangelism.

For we never came with words of flattery, as you know, nor with a pretext for greed—God is witness. (2:5)

The Thessalonians could testify that not a single word of flattery had come out of the mouth of the apostle, but God is the only true witness who can discern the real motives for human actions. "I the LORD search the heart and test the mind, to give every man according to his ways, according to the fruit of his deeds" (Jeremiah 17:10). As a faithful servant wrote, "Absolute loyalty to the truth must take the first place in the life of every servant of God." Truth is absolute and requires absolute loyalty.

Nor did we seek glory from people, whether from you or from others, though we could have made demands as apostles of Christ. (2:6)

Human glory is like the flower of the grass: "the grass withers and the flower falls" (1 Pet. 1:24). Servants have fallen into the trap of the glory that comes from men and, at times, from Christians. The only glory of the servant of God is the approval of his Master. Paul went further by refusing to be paid by the Thessalonians. Nothing was to be an obstacle to communicating the word of the Lord which is to remain forever (1 Pet. 1:25).

c. *Characteristics of the evangelist (2:7-12)*

But we were gentle among you, like a nursing mother taking care of her own children. (2:7)

One of the characteristics of the Lord's servant should be his kindness to everyone (see 2 Tim. 2:24). Paul uses the example of a nursing mother who shows gentleness when she takes care of the little children entrusted to her, actually her own children. This illustration of the character of Paul's presence in the midst of these young believers shows his affection for them. We also think of the touching affection of Christ for His Church, which He nourishes and cherishes (the same verb in Greek as in the case of the nursing mother) (Eph. 5:29).

So, being affectionately desirous of you, we were ready to share with you not only the gospel of God but also our own selves, because you had become very dear to us. (2:8)

17

This is how far the affection of Paul and his companions for these young believers went: they were willing to lay down their lives for them. But we know of One greater than Paul who, "having loved his own who were in the world, he loved them to the end" (John 13:1). It was for lost sinners that Jesus, in His love, voluntarily gave His life on the cross. It is always precious for each one of us to remember that "the Son of God loved me and gave himself for me" (Gal. 2:20). The servant of God is ready to place his goods and resources at the disposal of his Master; he is ready to even give his life if this is the will of the Lord.

For you remember, brothers, our labor and toil: we worked night and day, that we might not be a burden to any of you, while we proclaimed to you the gospel of God. (2:9)

Fourteen times in the first letter to the Thessalonians and seven times in the second, Paul addresses believers belonging to the church as "brothers". For us Christians, this is our title of nobility. Our freedom to use it among ourselves comes from the fact that the Lord Jesus Himself calls us His brothers (John 20:17). But the Lord is "the firstborn among many brothers" (Rom. 8:29) and, for this reason, it would be irreverent to call Him our brother. He is *our Lord*.

Paul, therefore, reminds his brothers that even though he had preached the gospel to them, his hands were not idle. As in the case of the Corinthians, being "free from all" in regard to his material needs, Paul says that he had made himself "a servant to all, that I might win more of them" (1 Cor. 9:19). In making tents (Act. 18:3), his hands ministered not only to his necessities, but also to those who were with him (Act. 20:34). In 2 Thessalonians 3, Paul is also able to rebuke with moral authority those who walked in disorder by not working at all and meddled in everything.

You are witnesses, and God also, how holy and righteous and blameless was our conduct toward you believers. (2:10)

This verse further explains why Paul could be imitated (1:6). Three aspects of his conduct are the objects of the Thessalonians' and God's witnessing. Firstly, his conduct was holy, i.e., separated from evil, and therefore it favored closeness to God. Secondly, righteousness characterized his relationships with men: his fellow men could not reproach him for any injustice. Thirdly, in regard to himself, as a servant who had received a particular service, he had nothing for which to blame or reproach himself. If we imitate such a model, God will be glorified by our conduct.

For you know how, like a father with his children, (2:11)

Earlier, we noticed that Paul used the image of a nursing mother to describe his affection for the Thessalonians. Here the image of a father suits the one who encourages, comforts, and gives reassurance of the things of God to each of his children. In our society, these responsibilities of a father, and even of a Christian father, are often left to the mother alone, when they are not simply ignored. We know the subsequent, harmful results for children. It is a very serious matter for every father to examine himself and to see to what extent he encourages, consoles, and even testifies before his children. It may also be that it is outside the family circle that God allows us to meet a soul who needs to be encouraged, comforted, edified by our testimony in order to continue on his or her path in a way worthy of God.

we exhorted each one of you and encouraged you and charged you to walk in a manner worthy of God, who calls you into his own kingdom and glory. (2:12)

The Ephesians are exhorted to walk in a manner worthy of the calling to which they have been called (Eph. 4:1). This calling goes back to eternity past, for God chose us in Christ before the foundation of the world. Paul will ask God that the Colossians might walk in a manner worthy of the Lord so that He might be pleased with them in every respect (Col. 1:10). This is obviously in relation to the present time on earth. Here the apostle wants to see the Thessalonians walk in a manner worthy of God in connection with the future and with eternity, for God calls us to share His own kingdom and glory. What a source of joy for the believer who has accepted God's Word to realize that such a heritage awaits him or her!

d. Reception of the Word and subsequent suffering (2:13-16)

And we also thank God constantly for this, that when you received the word of God, which you heard from us, you accepted it not as the word of men but as what it really is, the word of God, which is at work in you believers. (2:13)

We have just seen some characteristics of the gospel preached and of the evangelist himself. But what reception did the Thessalonians give to the Word of God? They received it as what it truly is, as inspired by God. The reception of this divine testimony defines what faith is. What assurance for the one who believes! We read in Psalm 19, verse 7: "The testimony of the Lord is sure." How effectively the evangelist has played his role! It was not his word that was received, but the very Word of God who used a man as an instrument to manifest His grace. The contact between God and the soul of the listener is now established. From then on, the Word of God works in the one who believes.

For you, brothers, became imitators of the churches of God in Christ Jesus that are in Judea. For you suffered the same things from your own countrymen as they did from the Jews, (2:14)

The Thessalonians, as we saw in chapter one, had become imitators of Paul, as well as of the Lord. Here we see that they had become imitators of the churches in Judea. We read that, as a result of a great persecution against the church in Jerusalem, "they were all scattered throughout the regions of Judea and Samaria, except the apostles"

(Acts 8:1). Paul recalls that brothers and sisters who had come out of Judaism had suffered at the hands of the Jews. The Thessalonians had endured similar sufferings at the hands of their compatriots.

But God, having first permitted these sufferings, had in His grace blessed the church of Thessalonica, so that like the churches in Judea, Galilee, and Samaria, it had peace, being built up and walking in the fear of the Lord and in the comfort of the Holy Spirit (Acts 9:31). Even today, many Christians still encounter opposition to their Christian faith on the part of their fellow citizens. The Lord Jesus is in a position to sympathize with them, for He lived through such suffering: "his own people did not receive him" (John 1:11), "not even his brothers believed in him" (John 7:5).

who killed both the Lord Jesus and the prophets, and drove us out, and displease God and oppose all mankind (2:15)

Paul rebukes the unbelieving Jews for five things. Firstly, they had put the Lord Jesus to death; Peter reminds them on the day of Pentecost: "you crucified and killed [him] by the hands of lawless men" (Acts 2:23). Secondly, they were responsible for the death of the prophets: the Lord had made a similar accusation against the hypocritical scribes and Pharisees and against Jerusalem, "the city that kills the prophets and stones those who are sent to it" (Matt. 23:37). Thirdly, they had persecuted Paul: obviously God had used these circumstances to allow the gospel to be proclaimed elsewhere, but the responsibility for persecuting God's envoys remained. Fourthly, the Jews are accused of not pleasing God; the Son of God, on the other hand, always did the things that were pleasing to the Father (John 8:29). The exhortation to please God is also addressed to us later in our epistle (4:1). Fifthly, they were opposed to all men in that they were hindering, as we shall see in the next verse, the preaching of the gospel.

by hindering us from speaking to the Gentiles that they might be saved—so as always to fill up the measure of their sins. But wrath has come upon them at last! (2:16)

The Jews refused to obey the gospel and hindered others from receiving it. This is all the more serious because in so doing they were protesting against an ordinance from God: "now he commands all people everywhere to repent" (Acts 17:30). The consequence of such opposition to God's work is that anger eventually reached them. At present, the Jews are, for the most part, scattered throughout the nations. In the future, God will use the Antichrist and the Assyrian (1 John 2:18 and Isaiah 7:17) to punish them in their own country. The Antichrist, or the other beast (Rev. 13:11-18), will be the enemy from within; the Assyrian, the rod of God's wrath (Isaiah 10:5), will be the enemy from without. But God will pour out a spirit of grace and supplication on His people Israel, and the inhabitants of the land will turn to their rejected Messiah (Zechariah 12:8-14). God will not abandon His earthly people.

e. *Paul's desire to see the Thessalonians again (2:17-20).*

But since we were torn away from you, brothers, for a short time, in person not in heart, we endeavored the more eagerly and with great desire to see you face to face, (2:17)

Paul had only been in Thessaloniki for about three weeks. But this short period of time had been sufficient for close bonds of affection to develop between him and the Thessalonians. Like a nursing mother taking care of her own children, he had taken care of them; like a father, he had encouraged them. And now their physical absence was painful for him, although in his heart he was not separated from them. How greatly he must have desired to see them again! But he had been prevented from doing so.

because we wanted to come to you—I, Paul, again and again—but Satan hindered us. (2:18)

When the Holy Spirit had prevented Paul from proclaiming the Word in Asia and from going to Bithynia (see Acts 16:6, 7), the result elsewhere was the conversion of souls in several cities, including Thessalonica. In this verse, we see the Adversary, for this is what the word Satan means, preventing Paul on two occasions from going to the Thessalonians. We know that one form of Satan's activity is to oppose the brothers by standing up as an accuser against them (Rev. 12:10). In a day to come, his activity will manifest itself in the operation of miracles, signs, and wonders of lies by the lawless one (2 Thes. 2:8, 9). On the other hand, it is comforting to know that the God of peace will soon crush Satan under our feet (Rom. 16:20).

For what is our hope or joy or crown of boasting before our Lord Jesus at his coming? Is it not you? (2:19)

We find in this verse the only question Paul asks in his letter. Its purpose is undoubtedly to attract the attention of his readers in Thessalonica. "See", he says, in connection with this future day of the coming of the Lord, "you are my hope, my joy, my crown." On the subject of hope, we read that Christ Jesus is our hope (1 Tim. 1:1). The fact that the Thessalonians are Paul's hope and his crown suggests, perhaps, that with the blessed hope of seeing Christ at His coming, there is also a very special glory reserved for those who will have been instruments in God's hands to convert and encourage souls.

For you are our glory and joy. (2:20)

Paul's glory and joy are not only related to the coming of the Lord. The Thessalonians were also a subject of glory and joy for the apostle. Paul will address those in Philippi in similar terms: "My brothers, whom I love and long for, my joy and crown" (Phil. 4:1). How happy it is for the heart of the faithful servant to glory and rejoice in those who are the fruit of his labor in the Lord!

It is on this happy note that we conclude the second section of our study. Paul, during his stay, had been able to encourage the believers in Thessalonica. Already he was rewarded by learning about the conduct of the Thessalonians who walked in a way worthy of God. He was now waiting to be glorified by the Lord at the time of His coming, in connection with the fruit of his labor. How could we not anticipate that wonderful day when Christ, the perfect Servant, shall see the fruit of the anguish of His soul and be satisfied (Isaiah 53:11)!

III

NEWS FROM TIMOTHY

Chapter 3

Thus, Paul had greatly longed to see his beloved brothers and sisters again, but was prevented from doing so by Satan. We will see in this third section of our study, corresponding to the third chapter of Paul's letter, that he had sent Timothy to inquire about the state of the Thessalonians. Timothy had returned with good news about their faith and love. Encouraged, Paul could then give thanks and persevere in prayer for his brothers and sisters in Christ.

a. *Sending Timothy (3:1-5)*

Therefore when we could bear it no longer, we were willing to be left behind at Athens alone, (3:1)

Certainly, in a foreign city like Athens, the presence of a Timothy or Silas would have been of great comfort to the apostle Paul. But love does not insist on its own way (1 Cor. 13:5). If it is true that Paul was controlled by the love of Christ (2 Cor. 5:14), it is also true that he loved the brothers and the sisters to the point of not caring about himself. Such love is more powerful than the obstacles raised by Satan: if Paul could not go to Thessalonica himself, he was going to send another brother.

and we sent Timothy, our brother and God's coworker in the gospel of Christ, to establish and exhort you in your faith, (3:2).

In their service for the Lord, Timothy and Paul were closely linked. Timothy was not just a "brother", but "our brother"; he was not just any "servant", but "our fellow worker under God" (as it is expressed in some translations). It was from such a brother that Paul agreed to part for the more pressing interests of the Thessalonians. Previously, Timothy had done the work of an evangelist, but now he was called to do the work of a teacher by strengthening souls and that of a shepherd by encouraging souls. Timothy means "dear to God." May God, in His grace, continue to give us servants who are dear to Him, capable of instructing us while encouraging us and encouraging us while instructing us!

that no one be moved by these afflictions. For you yourselves know that we are destined for this. (3:3)

The Thessalonians, as we have already seen, had received the Word of God with great trials that resulted in suffering at the hands of their own people. Paul's heart was not insensitive to this, knowing full well that the Enemy can use these trials to shake the faith of young believers. How is it that we are destined to undergo trials? Paul, in a letter to Timothy, wrote that all who wish to live a godly life in Christ Jesus will be persecuted (2 Tim. 3:12). To live godly means to live for God and His interests, which a person who is not born again cannot understand or accept. Trials, therefore, are frequently the part of those who want to honor the Lord in their Christian walk.

For when we were with you, we kept telling you beforehand that we were to suffer affliction, just as it has come to pass, and just as you know. (3:4)

Paul had hidden nothing from the new believers in Thessalonica. They had learned from the apostle that they would undergo trials.

His preaching of the gospel was not intended to deceive, or to hide anything, in order to make new converts and thus gain personal glory. The Lord Himself speaks of those who suffer affliction. These afflictions in a world and by a world that has rejected Christ may be necessary so that we may not love this world, but that our eyes may be fixed on Him who is coming soon. He adds: "But take heart; I have overcome the world" (John 16:33). Peter reminds us that these trials are for a little while, if necessary, "so that the tested genuineness of your faith–more precious than gold that perishes though it is tested by fire–may be found to result in praise and glory and honor in the revelation of Jesus Christ" (1 Pet. 1:6, 7).

For this reason, when I could bear it no longer, I sent to learn about your faith, for fear that somehow the tempter had tempted you and our labor would be in vain. (3:5)

Paul uses this strong expression a second time in his letter: "For this reason, when I could bear it no longer". The first time ("Therefore, when we could bear it no longer" 3:1), in his desire to know the spiritual condition of the Thessalonians, he had chosen to be left alone in Athens. Here, with the same desire, he had decided to send Timothy to inquire about the state of their faith. Paul knows very well that this Church in God the Father and in the Lord Jesus Christ can be guarded by the power of God. But he does not underestimate the power of Satan, the tempter, and the damage he can cause by attacking the faith of the believers. It is proper for the servant not only to fulfill the service that the Lord has entrusted to him, but also to be concerned about the fruit that will result from this service.

b. *Good news from Timothy (3:6-8)*

But now that Timothy has come to us from you, and has brought us the good news of your faith and love and reported that you always remember us kindly and long to see us, as we long to see you— (3:6)

27

This good news reported by Timothy must have calmed the apostle's anxiety, and also made him happy. The trials had not shaken the faith of the Thessalonians, nor cooled their love. It is true that there were difficulties concerning their hope; Paul will deal with this later. However, not only did they still have good memories of Paul, but they longed to see him again. It was a great encouragement for Paul to know that the Thessalonians shared his affection for them and that they persevered in faith and love.

for this reason, brothers, in all our distress and affliction we have been comforted [or encouraged] about you through your faith. (3:7)

We know that Paul was constantly concerned about the state of all the churches: it preoccupied him every day (2 Cor. 11:28), in spite of his own perils. Because the faith of the Thessalonians had not been shaken, Paul was encouraged. He knew very well that Satan attacks the faith of believers, especially the faith of young believers (v. 5). He had therefore sent Timothy to encourage them in this matter (v. 2). The news of their faith, reported by Timothy, has the effect of encouraging the apostle in return, in all his distress and affliction—no doubt his personal needs and trials.

For now we live, if you are standing fast in the Lord. (3. 8)

Paul could say that for him to live is Christ. But he also lived for those who belong to Christ. His concern about the young church in Thessalonica was so great that he was as dying, to use his expression elsewhere (2 Cor. 6:9). Now following the good news reported by Timothy, he was alive again (literally: he lived). But the apostle does not stop there. He now enjoins them to stand firm in the Lord, no doubt in the midst of trials; in his second letter he encourages them to stand firm, or to persevere, in his teachings (2 Thes. 2:15).

c. *Thanksgiving and prayers (3:9-13)*

For what thanksgiving can we return to God for you, for all the joy that we feel for your sake before our God, (3:9)

Once his fears are allayed, not only can Paul live again, but he can give thanks to God who has preserved his beloved Thessalonians. It is as if there were not enough thanksgiving to show his gratitude to God for all the joy his brothers and sisters gave him. God Himself is witness to the joy with which Paul rejoices.

as we pray most earnestly night and day that we may see you face to face and supply what is lacking in your faith? (3:10)

At the end of his letter, Paul exhorts the Thessalonians to pray without ceasing (5:17). In this verse we see Paul praying constantly, night and day, but also urgently. And why such prayers? First of all, to see them again. Satan, we remember, had prevented him from going to them when he had sought to see them face to face (2:17, 18). Paul relied on God because he wanted to make up for what was lacking in their faith. What was lacking in their faith? Not love, for they longed to see him and were taught by God to love one another (3:6; 4:9). Of course, they could always increase and abound in love (3:12). But perhaps their hope was weak. We note that, in this chapter, Paul does not mention Timothy bringing any good news about hope. As indicated above, Paul will address this need a little later in his letter.

Now may our God and Father himself, and our Lord Jesus, direct our way to you, (3:11)

If the way was to be opened to return to Thessaloniki, it was to be opened by God Himself. Two things are remarkable in this short verse. First, Paul's dependence on his heavenly Father and his Lord to open the way. (In fact, the apostle will write the second letter to the Thessalonians before seeing them again). Then, as others have pointed out, there is the testimony given to the divinity of the Lord.

The verb of the sentence is indeed in the singular (in the original Greek), despite the two subjects. The Lord Jesus as God possesses both the same nature as the Father and a distinct personality. "In the beginning was the Word, and the Word was with God, and the Word was God." (John 1:1).

and may the Lord make you increase and abound in love for one another and for all, as we do for you, (3:12)

Paul's prayer for himself is that the Lord will open the way for him to see the Thessalonians again. His prayer for them is that the Lord will cause them to show more love. Not only to grow in love, but to abound in it. Christian standards are high, because our position is high! Paul wants them not only to love one another, but to exercise their love toward those who are not of the house of faith. The love that the Lord had produced in the apostle's heart for the Thessalonians is the model for strengthening their hearts.

so that he may establish your hearts blameless in holiness before our God and Father, at the coming of our Lord Jesus with all his saints. (3:13)

This third mention of the coming of the Lord Jesus is specifically His coming with the saints, not for the saints. The first return of the Lord for us, to come and seek us, is the blessed hope; His second return with us is the appearance of His glory (Titus 2:13: literally: "the blessed hope and manifestation of the glory of our great God and Savior Jesus Christ"). The pure grace of God is demonstrated in relation to the Lord's coming for us; our responsibility is set forth in relation to His coming with us. When He comes with us, we will appear with Him in glory (Col. 3:4).

But before that great event, we will have been manifested before the judgment seat of Christ in order to receive what is due, according to the deeds done in the body, whether good or evil (2 Cor. 5:10). In this manifestation, or appearance, before the judgment seat of Christ, it is not said that we will be judged, for Christ was judged in the place of the believer. Moreover, there is "therefore now no condemnation for those who are in Christ Jesus" (Rom. 8:1). As we await these manifestations, our responsibility is to tolerate nothing foreign to God's holiness in our lives.

∽o∽

Consideration of this last verse concludes our section. Paul introduces the idea of holiness which he will develop in chapter 4 of his letter. The subject of holiness is very important, as we shall see, in our Christian walk. On the one hand, God is honored to see this fruit of divine nature in His own people. On the other hand, the appreciation of truths such as the coming of the Lord for us goes hand in hand with a walk separated from the world and from evil.

Let us ask the Lord to dispose our hearts to walk with God, like Enoch, that man of faith. "By faith Enoch was taken up so that he should not see death, and he was not found, because God had taken him. Now before he was taken he was commended as having pleased God." (Heb. 11:5; see also Gen. 5:24).

IV

WALKING IN HOLINESS

Chapter 4, verses 1-12

The verses that are going to occupy us present important subjective truths for the believer who awaits the return of the Lord Jesus. They concern the Christian walk, in order to please God. If these truths are put into practice, they dispose the believer's heart to appreciate the objective truths that we will consider later, i.e., the events surrounding the coming of the Lord.

In the first twelve verses of the fourth chapter, Paul exhorts the Thessalonians with three commandments: with regard to God, to walk according to His will (vv. 3-8); with regard to brothers and sisters, to walk in brotherly love (vv. 9-10); with regard to those outside, to walk honorably (vv. 11-12).

But, first of all, Paul encourages the Thessalonians to abound in a walk that pleases God.

a. *Walking and pleasing God (4:1, 2)*

Finally, then, brothers, we ask and urge [or exhort] you in the Lord Jesus, that as you received from us how you ought to walk and to please God, just as you are doing, that you do so more and more. (4:1)

Paul had backed his teachings to the Thessalonians on the Christian walk by his own conduct: holy, righteous, and blameless (2:10) He recognized that their walk and their willingness to please God was good. If our walk, i.e., our Christian life, is pleasing to God, it will be a good witness to those around us. Now we are encouraged to make more progress before the Lord returns (3:13). Peter, on the other hand, in connection with the day of God, will exhort believers to live lives of holiness and godliness (2 Pet. 3:11-12). The Lord can and will truly encourage us to persevere in our earthly walk, in order to please God.

For you know what instructions we gave you through the Lord Jesus. (4:2)

Under the Old Covenant, i.e., the Law, all the commandments of God had to be observed; otherwise, a curse would fall on offenders (see Deut. 11:26-28). Thankfully, God, in His mercy, had provided for sacrifices that were offered continuously every year, but they could not make perfect those who draw near the altar (Heb. 10:1). The Lord Jesus offered Himself as a sacrifice for sins, and because of the excellence of His person and His sacrifice, the believer is now cleansed from all sin by the blood of Jesus Christ (1 John 1:7). In the present time of grace, observance of the instructions given by the Lord results from a motive which is no longer fear, but rather the love of our Savior: "Whoever has my commandments and keeps them, he it is who loves me" (John 14:21). The Thessalonians kept these instructions from the Lord that Paul had given them. The first instruction has to do with God.

b. *Walk according to God's will (4:3-8)*

For this is the will of God, your sanctification [or holiness]: that you abstain from sexual immorality; (4:3)

33

God is not at all indifferent to the way Christians behave in the world. Paul will weep when telling those in Philippi that many walk as enemies of the cross of Christ (Phil. 3:18). God wants to sanctify us, to separate us morally from the world and from everything that can defile us in this world. Notice the word holiness which is repeated in verses 4 and 7 of chapter 4 and verse 13 of chapter 3. We have to practically realize this position of holiness in which our faith in Jesus Christ has placed us. God desires us to share in His holiness. One instruction is to abstain from sexual immorality, one of the first works of the flesh (see Gal. 5:19). The following verse gives us another instruction.

that each one of you know how to control his own body in holiness and honor, (4:4).

Paul will remind the Corinthians that their bodies are members of Christ (1 Cor. 6:15). Our bodies are not meant for sexual immorality, but for the Lord, because we belong to Him. Moreover, they are, in the case of Christians, the temple of the Holy Spirit dwelling in them. We are therefore exhorted to glorify God in our bodies. See 1 Corinthians 6:13-20. In these verses it is not said to resist sexual immorality, but to flee from it. Note Joseph's conduct before the advances of his master's wife in Genesis 39: he refused (v. 8), he did not listen (v. 10), he fled (v. 12).

The Greek word for "body" means literally a "vessel" (*skeuos*) and could refer to the believer's wife, as in 1 Peter 3:7. So we could translate this verse: "that each one of you may know how to take a wife for himself in holiness and honor." Marriage is a safeguard against sexual immorality. Paul exhorts the Corinthians that every man should have his own wife, and every woman her own husband, because of sexual immorality (1 Cor. 7:2).

not in the passion of lust like the Gentiles who do not know God; (4:5).

The Christian finds that his knowledge of God distinguishes him from unbelieving people of the nations, who do not know God. His new nature enables him to discern sin and also the occasions that can lead to sin. On the one hand, sin is that which produces in us all kinds of covetousness (Rom. 7:8); on the other hand, covetousness (*epithumia*, also translated "lust"), having conceived, gives birth to sin (Jas. 1:15). Let us remember that we no longer belong to ourselves, doing as we please, for we have been bought at a price (1 Cor. 6:19, 20).

that no one transgress and wrong his brother in this matter, because the Lord is an avenger in all these things, as we told you beforehand and solemnly warned you. (4:6)

In pursuing this subject of holiness and abstaining from sexual immorality, Paul reminds us of the rights of the injured brother whose wife has been led into adultery. The Lord Himself could intervene by avenging that injured brother, whose brother had taken advantage of him. He could judge and even punish the latter brother, guilty of such a sin. At Corinth, some had been guilty of such immorality (1 Cor. 5:1). The Lord had intervened in discipline by the physical visitations of weakness, sickness, and death on believers who had committed such sins and had not judged themselves (1 Cor. 11:30-32).

For God has not called us for impurity, but in holiness. (4:7)

While the Lord looks after the interests of those who have been wronged, we are also responsible for giving an account of our actions to God who has called us to live a life of holiness. Our God is a holy God whose eyes are too pure to see evil (Habakkuk 1:13). When His Son was made sin at Golgotha (2 Cor. 5. 21), God turned His face away. It is important for us to appreciate God's holiness, as we too often treat the issue of sin lightly despite our Christian calling. If we do, we despise God.

Therefore whoever disregards this, disregards not man but God, who gives his Holy Spirit to you. (4:8)

This verse introduces another divine person: the Holy Spirit or the Spirit of holiness, as we read in Romans 1:4. God gave Him to dwell in us, as we mentioned earlier. God considers holiness important enough to give us a divine person to do this work in us. If we pursue our own lusts instead of practical holiness, we disregard (despise, reject, according to other translations) God. Let us not do so. Rather, like that faithful residue in the time of Malachi (chapter 4, verse 2), but with greater light, let us fear Him who has given us the gift of His Son and the Holy Spirit, walking according to His will and not ours.

c. *Walking in brotherly love (4:9, 10)*

Now concerning brotherly love you have no need for anyone to write to you, for you yourselves have been taught by God to love one another, (4:9)

Among God's people, we should encounter sincere brotherly love, the intrinsic response of the obedience of the truth (see 1 Pet. 1:22). This love for brothers and sisters is not learned from the world. It is taught by God. It is received with the new birth: "We know that we have passed out of death into life, because we love our brothers and sisters" (1 John 3:14). The Lord, in His love for us, calls us His brothers (John 20:17). He desires us to be true "Philadelphians," i.e., those who love the brothers.

for that indeed is what you are doing to all the brothers throughout Macedonia. But we urge [or exhort] you, brothers, to do this more and more, (4:10)

The Thessalonians' love for the brothers was not limited to just a few brothers and sisters in the local church. No, it extended to all the brothers in the region of Macedonia. What does brotherly love consist of? It is characterized by affection for one another (Rom. 12:10). In the Epistle to the Hebrews, we are exhorted to persevere in brotherly love (13:1); here, in our verse, we are exhorted to abound in it more and more. As we have seen before, it is the Lord who makes us grow and abound in love for one another.

d. *Walk honorably (4:11, 12)*

and to aspire to live quietly, and to mind your own affairs, and to work with your hands, as we instructed you, (4:11)

The exhortation of this verse aims at fostering a climate in which true brotherly love can develop. Restlessness rather than a quiet life, being occupied with the affairs of others rather than our own, and idleness rather than honest work: these are all obstacles which prevent us from cultivating brotherly love and which, unfortunately, can degenerate into excesses which dishonor God. Paul had encouraged the Thessalonians to apply themselves to living quietly, the result of minding their own affairs and working with their own hands. The verb "to apply oneself" has the meaning in Greek of being ambitious, of setting a precise goal. Effort is needed, then, but it is motivated by the desire to have a good testimony.

so that you may walk properly before outsiders and be dependent on no one. (4:12)

A quiet life, occupation with our own affairs, and working with our own hands produce, first of all, a good testimony to those of the world. Let us be assured that the latter know how to differentiate an honorable walk from one that is not in conformity with the Christian's calling. It is true that we recognize a Christian by his talk, but we distinguish him from other people by his walk. Secondly, we will be independent of others. In this, Paul is an example for us: he could have lived by the gospel (1 Cor. 9:14, 15), but he chose instead to work night and day so as not to be a burden to any of the Thessalonians (2:9).

In closing, we recall the two main subjective truths in this section that have occupied us: holiness in our walk and brotherly love for one another. We can only understand and appreciate the value of the truths about the coming of the Lord, which we will examine in the next section of our study and in the next chapter of this epistle, if our life honors the Lord and if we love our brothers and sisters.

V

THE COMING OF THE LORD

Chapter 4, verses 13-18

In this portion of Paul's letter to the Thessalonians, two objective truths are placed before us: the coming of the Lord with His own (v. 13, 14) and His coming for His own (v. 15-18). In order to understand more about the coming of the Lord *with* His own, we must read the first verses of chapter 5 and also the second letter to the Thessalonians. As for the Lord's coming *for* His own, or what is often called "the rapture", verses 15-18 are most instructive as well as those in 1 Corinthians 15.

We will see that the teachings concerning the coming of the Lord transmitted by the apostle Paul are intended to calm the concern of the Thessalonians regarding deceased brothers and sisters. These worried believers will be encouraged by the precious truths that will be revealed to them.

a. *The Coming of the Lord with His own (4:13, 14)*

But we do not want you to be uninformed, brothers, about those who are asleep, that you may not grieve as others do who have no hope. (4:13)

As we read this verse, we discern a particular concern among the young believers in Thessalonica about those who had fallen asleep— it is the expression the Word of God uses concerning dead believers. Of course, they were distressed to see loved ones leaving them. But that is not what Paul is referring to here. They were grieved that, having received and accepted this truth of the Lord's return, the brothers and sisters who had fallen asleep in the Lord would not enjoy this great event of the Lord's coming with all the saints. But we will see that they did not possess all the truth about the coming of the Lord: at the very least, they were ignorant about those who had fallen asleep. The apostle will strengthen their hope by shedding light on these truths of the coming of the Lord *with* His people and *for* His people.

For since we believe that Jesus died and rose again, even so, through Jesus, God will bring with him those who have fallen asleep (4:14)

To understand this verse, we must realize that it relates to the first verses of chapter 5. It refers to the day of the Lord, when He will come to exercise His judgment against a rebellious world, to be glorified in His saints and admired in those who believe (2 Thes. 1:7-10). Then we will accompany Him. Let us note that it is God who brings (brings back, in other translations) with Jesus those who have fallen asleep in Him. We can believe in this coming event as surely as we believe in the death and resurrection of the Lord.

The following verses give us details about the resurrection of Christians when the Lord Jesus comes first for His own—this is the rapture. Some time later (most likely seven years) God will then bring these resurrected believers, as well as those who were alive at the time of the rapture, with the Lord in His day. He will come to establish His millennial reign of peace on earth.

b. *The Lord's coming for His own (4:15-18)*

For this we declare to you by a word from the Lord, that we who are alive, who are left until the coming of the Lord, will not precede those who have fallen asleep. (4:15)

The expression "a word from the Lord" means a special revelation to Paul that gives him authority to present the following teachings about the coming of the Lord for His own people, i.e., the rapture. Let us note in verses 15 to 18 the five expressions related to this title of Lord: a word from the Lord, the coming of the Lord, the Lord Himself, to meet the Lord, to be with the Lord. Let us not lose sight of the first place that the Lord will have at this happy moment of the rapture of the Church. Our true hope is to see Him soon when we will go to meet Him.

Therefore, we are happy to be informed about the events that will take place on the occasion of the rapture of the Church. The apostle instructs us about the living who will remain until this first coming of the Lord; they will not be brought into the presence of the Lord before those who have fallen asleep. In a way, the dead in Christ will precede the living by being raised first. All believers will go together to meet the Lord.

For the Lord himself will descend from heaven with a cry of command, with the voice of an archangel, and with the sound of the trumpet of God. And the dead in Christ will rise first. (4:16)

The Lord Himself will come down from heaven to take His own. He has already come to this earth and men have rejected Him. He came down to the lower parts of the earth, i.e., death, but He also ascended far above all the heavens (Eph. 4:9, 10). This joy of coming to seek His own belongs to Him. What a glorious and touching moment when the believers of the Church and the saints of the Old Testament will meet the Lord!

The three instruments used by the Lord to call His own suggest, indeed, that the Church will not be called alone. Of course, the cry of the Bridegroom will be heard for the Beloved: Christ desires to present the Church to Himself, glorious, without spot or wrinkle—or any such thing (Eph. 5:27). Christ is the head of the Church (Eph. 1:22; Col. 1:18): His cry is a cry of commandment. As for Israel, we see the angels playing an important role in their national history. The law itself had been ordained, or administered, by angels (Gal. 3:19). For the saints of Israel, therefore, the Lord will use the voice of the archangel. Finally, all the others who have died in the faith—Abel, Noah, Job, Ruth, Naaman, etc.—will be summoned by the trumpet of God.

Following this irresistible call of the Lord, the dead will be raised. Not all the dead, but the dead in Christ. It is not the dead according to the family of Adam, but those who have known the new birth during their lifetime who will be the first to experience the power of this life that dwells in the Son of God. Having passed through death on the earth, they will know the power of resurrection in a similar way to their Lord. It is a blessed consolation for us who are left on earth to know that those who have gone before us will experience what the Lord has undergone: after death, the resurrection of the body which will join the soul and the spirit.

What encouragement for the Christians of Thessalonica to learn that the dead would lose nothing at the coming of the Lord, but that they would be the first to experience this power when He returns! They no longer had reason to grieve, for they now had a living hope.

Then we who are alive, who are left, will be caught up together with them in the clouds to meet the Lord in the air, (4:17a)

Those who are dead, therefore, are the first to answer the Lord's call. Then the living who remain on the earth also answer it. There will, therefore, be believers on the earth when the Lord returns. Our generation may very well be the one that will see the return of the Lord. Our Master could summon us into His presence today! Do we truly believe this momentous truth?

Some would like to deprive us of the joy of going to meet the Lord very soon by suggesting several raptures. They do not know the heart of the Lord. "We will be raptured together" excludes the idea of more than one rapture. "Together" means both the dead in Christ and all the believers present on earth at the Lord's return. In addition, we are encouraged to wait for the Lord at any time. The Lord's promise "I am coming soon" is repeated three times in the last chapter of Revelation.

Where will the meeting take place? In the clouds. The world that rejects Christ will not witness this wonderful moment when all the redeemed will be taken into the presence of the Lord Jesus who will come for them. Let us remember that He Himself, when He was lifted up from the earth, was received in a cloud, which carried Him away from before the eyes of His own people (Acts 1:9). The world had no knowledge of His elevation from the earth. Later, He will return with the clouds, and then "every eye will see him" (Rev. 1:7). This will be His coming with His own.

Our verse further specifies that we will meet Him in the air. We know that the principalities, the authorities, the rulers of darkness, the spiritual powers of wickedness are in heavenly places (Eph. 6:12). Satan Himself is there (Luke 10:18; Rev. 12:7-9). These are the places that the Lord has chosen to meet His redeemed ones. He will thus manifest His authority and glorious power over the enemy of our souls!

and so we will always be with the Lord. (4:17b)

Many believers say that their happiness will be to go to heaven. What the Word of God says about the believer's happiness is even more wonderful. To the repentant criminal on the cross, Jesus said, "Truly, I say to you, today you will be with me in paradise" (Luke 23:43). It was true that this criminal would go to heaven, but his true happiness would be to be there with Jesus.

For us too, this blessed prospect has not changed: we will soon be with the Lord. Perhaps today... Not only that, but we will always be with the Lord. There will be nothing to distract our gaze from the Beloved, or to make our affection for Him lukewarm. For all eternity in the Father's house, we will worship and pay homage to the One who gave His life for us.

Therefore encourage one another with these words. (4:18)

Truths about the Lord Jesus' return to take His own to Himself are a source of encouragement in this world. It is comforting to think that we will meet the Lord with all our brothers and sisters, sleeping in Him or alive, that Satan will not be able to hinder this event, unique in all history, and that we will always be with the Lord for all eternity.

It is good to encourage one another with these words, for often any one of us can lose sight of the blessed hope because of the worries and concerns of this life. Let us often remind one another, brothers and sisters, that Jesus is coming soon according to His promise. This hope will keep us from the world and all its artifices, and will prepare us, during the night, to await the Morning Star, the Lord Jesus Himself.

VI

THE DAY OF THE LORD

Chapter 5, verses 1-11

Verses 15 to 18 of chapter 4 form a kind of parenthesis; they describe the events surrounding the Lord's coming to gather believers. Chapter 5 is a continuation of the topic that Paul introduced immediately before these verses, about the fact that God will bring back those who have fallen asleep through Jesus. It concerns the Lord's manifestation to the world with the believers. This particular event is known in the Word of God as the day of the Lord.

Verses 1 to 3 in chapter 5 of Paul's letter deal with the Lord's day. From verse 4 to verse 7, we will see our privileged position as sons of light and, consequently, our responsibility not to sleep, but to put on the breastplate of faith and love and the helmet of salvation. Finally, in verses 9 to 11, we will consider what God has set before us, and we will be encouraged to edify one another.

a. *The Lord's Day (5:1-3)*

Now concerning the times and the seasons, brothers, you have no need to have anything written to you. (5:1)

We find the expression "times and seasons" three times in the Bible. In Daniel 2:21, it is God who changes times and seasons. In Acts. 1:7, concerning the restoration of the kingdom for Israel, it is the Father who has fixed times and seasons by His own authority. And here in our verse, the times and seasons are presented in relation to the day of the Lord. This expression is used in connection with the earth and its inhabitants.

The Church, as one hymn says, is now a stranger here on earth. Considered to be outside of time and seasons, it is heavenly. Its Head is glorified in heaven (Col. 1:18; Eph. 1:20-23). Its members were chosen before the foundation of the world in Christ (Eph. 1:3, 4). They are seen as seated together in the heavenly places in Christ Jesus (Eph. 2:6). Their present citizenship is heavenly and they await the Lord Jesus who will transform their bodies into a glorious body like His (Phil. 3:20, 21).

For you yourselves are fully aware that the day of the Lord will come like a thief in the night. (5:2)

In this verse, two things characterize the day of the Lord: it is a terrible day—the simile of a thief is evoked—and it is a day of darkness—the night is mentioned. The Thessalonians well knew this. We read in the book of the prophet Joel: "The day of the Lord is great and very awesome; who can endure it?" (2:11); and also, that it is "a day of darkness and gloom, a day of clouds and thick darkness" (2:2). Amos, another prophet, said to the house of Israel, "Woe to you who desire the day of the Lord! Why would you have the day of the Lord? It is darkness, and not light" (Amos 5:18).

The following verses in our chapter clearly show that Christians need not fear the coming of that day. They have the promise of the Lord: "I will keep you from the hour of trial that is coming on the whole world" (Rev. 3:10). Like the apostle John in Revelation chapter 4, we will have ascended into heaven beforehand, and we will see what will happen on earth from the glory above. To know more about the day of the Lord, we must carefully read Paul's second letter to the Thessalonians. The saints in that day will be with the Lord (see Zechariah 14:5 and Col. 3:4). The Lord will be glorified in His saints and admired in all who have believed (2 Thes. 1:10).

While people are saying, "There is peace and security," then sudden destruction will come upon them as labor pains come upon a pregnant woman, and they will not escape. (5:3)

Under the dominion of the Beast, who will be given "authority over every tribe and people and language and nation" (Rev. 13:7), it seems that the world will enjoy a certain peace. Already many are convinced that world peace will soon be achieved. Moreover, and this is apparent today, the world will feel increasingly secure in the face of supernatural events. There is less and less fear of such phenomena. People reject the idea of any intervention by God in human affairs, not to say that they simply do not fear God and even deny His existence. What a tragic delusion, which has its source in Satan, the father of lies! Sudden destruction will come upon those who are the object of such seduction.

Israel, the woman of Revelation 12:1-6, has already given birth to a son, a male child, who is to feed the nations, and who has been caught up to God and to His throne. This is the Lord Jesus, the Son of God. Israel will be kept in the wilderness in a place prepared by God and fed for three and a half years. This suggests God's providential care for a faithful remnant of Israel during the great tribulation. But the world is like a pregnant woman who cannot avoid the pains of natural childbirth: it will not escape the terrible judgments of a holy and righteous God.

The Christian, on the other hand, has nothing to fear. Christ Himself is his peace (Eph. 2:14) and stability (Isaiah 33:6). As the world seeks peace at all costs and deludes itself about its safety, the Christian knows that Christ did everything on the cross and rejoices in it. The peace and security of the Christian is not only for the present time, but for all eternity.

b. *Privilege and Responsibility (5:4-8)*

But you are not in darkness, brothers, for that day to surprise you like a thief. (5:4)

This verse, which begins with a "but", establishes the distinction between the believer and the unbeliever. Believers are not in darkness. It literally enveloped the world when Christ on the cross bore our sins during three hours (see Matt. 27:45, 46) and was made sin in our place. Moral darkness has persisted to this day in this world that still rejects Christ and His work of redemption. As in the case of the thief who prefers darkness in order to steal, so the day of the Lord will surprise the world in darkness. But for Christians, as for the sons of Israel in the land of Goshen (see Exodus 10:21-23), there is light in their dwellings even though moral darkness envelops the world.

For you are all children of light, children of the day. We are not of the night or of the darkness. (5:5)

On the first day of creation, God separated the light from the darkness. "God called the light Day, and the darkness he called Night" (Genesis 1:5). This important distinction in nature is also found in the moral sphere. The believer is considered as being of light and of day; the unbeliever is considered as being of darkness and of night. The Lord is truly the first Man who manifested this character of light, i.e., of holiness; but He was not understood and was not received by those who are of darkness (see John 1:1-13). As for us, God sent His Son to redeem us and adopt us; we are sons and heirs of God (Gal. 4:4-6). So, this divine character of holiness is now imprinted upon us. Before our conversion we were of the night and of the darkness like Satan; now we are of light and of day like Christ.

So then let us not sleep, as others do, but let us keep awake and be sober. (5:6)

In the Christian life, every privilege comes with a responsibility for the believer. In verses 4 and 5, we have seen that we are not in darkness, that we are sons of light and that we are not of the night and darkness. In verse 6, therefore, our responsibility follows: unlike unbelievers who sleep spiritually, believers are called to watch and be sober. They are called to watch, for they are waiting to see the Lord Jesus appear soon as the Morning Star, before the day dawns. They are called to be sober, for otherwise they would tarnish the Christian testimony before they are removed from this earthly scene to be brought into their heavenly homeland. What a responsibility to the Lord and to those who have not believed the gospel!

For those who sleep, sleep at night, and those who get drunk, are drunk at night. (5:7)

Morally speaking, in this world it is night; those of this world are sleeping. They have no spiritual motive to keep awake. Intoxication in its various forms, for instance, only introduces an individual deeper into the darkness of the moral night. We, Christians, are not exempt from the possibility of falling into this state of sleep and intoxication. The sinful nature in us is the same as that of unbelievers. But, thanks be to God, we have resources at our disposal.

But since we belong to the day, let us be sober, having put on the breastplate of faith and love, and for a helmet the hope of salvation. (5:8)

Those who are of the day, the Christians, must be sober, especially with regard to their bodies. As for their souls, they must protect their affection for the Lord Jesus by putting on the breastplate of faith and love. The hope of salvation is like a helmet for their spirit, keeping their thoughts fixed on the One they wait for during the

49

night and on the things that are above, not on the things that are on earth (Col. 3:2). As in chapter 1, verse 3, these three qualities of the Christian life—faith, love, and hope—are mentioned together. May these virtues of the Thessalonians, precious to the Lord, be found in our lives as we await the One who is coming soon!

c. *God's plan for us (5:9-11)*

For God has not destined us for wrath, but to obtain salvation through our Lord Jesus Christ, (5:9)

The book of Revelation describes the manifestation of God's wrath against this ungodly world by means of seven seals, seven trumpets, and seven vials. Because of His holiness, God must judge this world which rejected and killed His Son. However, the believer is not destined for wrath: these terrible judgments will not reach him, for Christ has already secured deliverance by giving His life. Our verse and that of Rom. 8:1 quoted earlier, "There is therefore now no condemnation for those who are in Christ Jesus," reassure us as to our standing in the face of God's judgments on this earth.

The question of God's wrath has been resolved for the believer in the past: "God has not destined us for wrath." Christ has suffered God's wrath in our place. For unbelievers, even if it is not yet felt, God's wrath is now upon them: "The wrath has come upon them at last" (2:16). As for the wrath that will be felt in the future, we need not fear: "Jesus delivers us from the wrath to come" (1:10).

who died for us so that whether we are awake or asleep we might live with him. (5:10)

The Thessalonians were concerned about being separated, at the coming of the Lord, from those among them who had already fallen asleep, i.e., who were dead. Here Paul writes about those who have fallen asleep in Jesus (4:14) or, if one prefers, the dead in Christ (4:16), in contrast to those who walk in this world without possessing the life of God (5:6, 7). Paul had already encouraged them by telling them that the believers on earth and the dead in Christ would be caught up together in the clouds to meet the Lord in the air (4:17). In our verse it goes further: not only will we be raptured together, but we will live together with the Lord. Rapture is the means to His end, i.e., to have us always with Him. This is a precious source of encouragement for each of us.

Therefore encourage one another and build one another up, just as you are doing. (5:11)

We are exhorted to talk about these things concerning the Lord's manifestation to the world, but also about proper behavior while awaiting the Lord, i.e., being watchful and sober. Discussing such matters is not reserved only for a few older brothers and sisters or those who are more knowledgeable of the Word of God. We are all called to edify one another. This is what the young believers of the church in Thessalonica were doing.

The coming of the Lord for us and His coming with us are truths about which the Holy Spirit has preserved many verses in the Bible. Knowing and appreciating these unique events should have two practical results in our lives. The light of our testimony should be such that it shines in the darkness to the glory of God, so that He can use it to awaken souls who are perishing and to encourage others who belong to Him. Moreover, we should already be rejoicing at the thought that soon we will be for eternity in the presence of Him who loved us and gave Himself up for us. May our Lord Himself give us to be encouraged by these precious truths of His coming!

VII

PAUL'S EXHORTATIONS TO THE BROTHERS

Chapter 5, verses 12-28

In these last verses of Paul's first letter to the Thessalonians, the apostle addresses about twenty exhortations to the believers in Thessalonica. These instructions can be grouped as follows: in relation to church life (v. 12-14), to Christian life in general (v. 15-18), to the activity of the Holy Spirit (v. 19-22). The epistle ends with the recommendations to God and final exhortations (v. 22-28).

It is always with the freedom of a brother in Christ towards his brothers and sisters that Paul addresses those of Thessalonica. These exhortations or instructions, here again, are intended to encourage the saints with convincing words. Verses 23 and 24 occupy a special place in the midst of these exhortations: Paul commends these young believers to God Himself to be kept blameless. We are weak, it is true, but God is there to help and support us as we await the return of the Lord Jesus.

a. *Church life (5:12-14)*

We ask you, brothers, to respect those who labor among you and are over you in the Lord and admonish you, (5:12)

We do not read that Paul had established brothers responsible for certain functions in the church of Thessalonica. It was simply a matter of recognizing certain brothers whom the Lord had called to serve Him. Three things characterized these brothers: they worked in the midst of the local church, they had spiritual authority, evidenced by giving direction, and they admonished their brothers and sisters. These leading brothers (see also Rom. 12:8), were motivated simply by the desire to be useful to the Lord as His instruments for the good of the church. They were to be held in high esteem.

and to esteem them very highly in love because of their work. Be at peace among yourselves. (5:13)

It is true that the worker deserves his food (Matt. 10:10), and that the one who is taught in the Word must share all temporal goods with the one who teaches (Gal. 6:6). But it is not to these principles of God applicable to servants that the apostle calls our attention here. If it is appropriate for us to have open hands, it is also appropriate for us to have open hearts towards the faithful servants in the Church. There are brothers and sisters who serve the Lord on a permanent basis, and others who have kept secular work and who also serve the Lord. God knows how much each one is rewarded for their dedication with a word of encouragement from their brothers and sisters. It is important to learn about the work of these servants, to pray for them, and to show them our esteem in love.

Peace among the members of a local church is conducive to our recognizing the moral authority of those whom the Lord has placed over us. All feelings of jealousy, pride and self-interest, rather than the interests of Jesus Christ (Phil. 2:21), are set aside. Then we esteem very highly in love those who devote themselves to the Lord and His local church. Peace also characterized the churches of Judea, Galilee, and Samaria. It may be thought that it was because of such a favorable climate that they were built up, walked in the fear of the Lord, and grew in the consolation of the Holy Spirit (Acts 9:31).

And we urge [or exhort] you, brothers, admonish the idle [or disorderly], encourage the fainthearted, help the weak, be patient with them all. (5:14)

This verse presents two important principles for the proper functioning of a Christian gathering. First, such a gathering should not be a collection of people doing whatever they want. It is important to know how to conduct oneself in the Church of the living God (1 Tim. 3:15): one must first warn those who are out of order, i.e., those who live in a disorderly manner.

Secondly, our concern for souls must be such that we seize the opportunities given by the Lord to console and help. In the cave of Adullam, David had received all those who had come to Him: people in distress, in debt, with bitterness in their souls (1 Samuel 22:1, 2). Such brothers and sisters can be found today. For those who perhaps have difficulty in knowing how to care for brothers and sisters who are disorderly, discouraged or weak, there are always opportunities to show patience towards all.

Finally, and this is another important responsibility, Paul's exhortation is directed to all brothers and sisters, not just to those who are over us. Let us ask the Lord to help us to exercise these different services for Him and for the saints in the Church of God.

b. *The Christian life (5:15-18)*

See that no one repays anyone evil for evil, but always seek to do good to one another and to everyone. (5:15)

Grace elevates above the principles and practices accepted in the world. While it is often natural and acceptable in our society to return evil for evil, we must be careful not to engage in such behavior. But to leave it at that would make us simply religious people. We must, moreover, pursue what is good. Such a practice extends not only to the Christians around us, but to all men. Elsewhere we are exhorted to pursue righteousness (1 Tim. 6:11; 2 Tim. 2:22), love (1 Cor. 14:1), peace (Heb. 12:14; 1 Pet. 3:11), and the things that tend towards peace and edification (Rom. 14:19). Our seeking to do good must be marked by perseverance: "always seek."

Rejoice always, (5:16)

This exhortation of the apostle, as well as those that follow, is intended to encourage the Christian in his journey toward heaven. By making these words ours, not only will our individual lives be transformed, but also our Christian gatherings will be transformed. We are encouraged to always rejoice. This cannot be the joy that the world brings, because such joy depends on various circumstances. As one hymn says, it can only be "that excellent joy which your Spirit, Jesus, puts in a heart." This joy, especially the joy of seeing the Lord Jesus soon, cannot be taken away from us (John 16:22).

The Holy Spirit, through the letters of Paul, encourages us to rejoice in the Lord (Phil. 3:1; 4:4) and with those who rejoice (Rom. 12:15). Even to the Corinthians, to whom Paul had to speak as to people of the flesh (1 Cor. 3:1), but who had repented, the apostle could later write: "Finally, brothers, rejoice. Aim for restoration, comfort one another, agree with one another, live in peace; and the God of love and peace will be with you" (2 Cor. 13:11).

pray without ceasing, (5:17)

If reading and meditating on the Bible are the food of the Christian, prayer is the breath of his soul. What characterizes prayer? We can learn from the Lord in Gethsemane in Luke 22:39-46.

1. He had a customary place to pray: "He went to the Mount of Olives as was his custom".
2. He prayed alone: "He withdrew from the disciples about a stone's throw".
3. He was dependent: "He knelt down".

4. He prayed aloud: "He prayed, saying".
5. He addressed His Father: "Father, if you are willing...".
6. He sought His will: "Not my will, but yours, be done".
7. He prayed intensely: "He prayed more earnestly."

What a lesson from the divine Master, and what a model for us! Let us ask the Lord to help us to persevere in prayer and to be watchful in it with thanksgiving (Col. 4:2).

give thanks in all circumstances; for this is the will of God in Christ Jesus for you. (5:18)

If we rejoice in the joy of the Lord and have communion with God in prayer, we can be assured that there will be no lack of subjects for thanksgiving. It is true that it can be difficult to give thanks in all things, but it is still God's will for us. Even if this is not always our perception, "we know that for those who love God all things work together for good, for those who are called according to his purpose" (Rom. 8:28). Often we perceive things as through a semi-transparent glass: we see dimly (1 Cor. 13:12). But in glory we will understand that our circumstances, even the most difficult, were given for our good by a God of love and wisdom. We can already give thanks in all things.

c. *The Activity of the Holy Spirit (5:19-22)*

Do not quench the Spirit. (5:19)

Regarding the Holy Spirit of God, we read that the believers should not grieve Him (Eph. 4:30); Israel had been guilty of such behavior (Isaiah 63:10). The Thessalonians, on the other hand, are exhorted not to quench the Spirit, i.e., not to act in such a way that the manifestation of the power of the Holy Spirit is hindered in the midst of the local church. He must correct us, help us to put our lives in order, and then enrich us with spiritual and other blessings.

Do not despise prophecies, (5:20)

At the beginning of the Church, before the books of the New Testament were written, prophecies were new revelations made by the Holy Spirit to Christians for the edification of other brothers and sisters. The word of prophecy today consists of a message presented by a brother under the guidance of the Holy Spirit, giving God's thought on a particular subject, according to the circumstances of the moment, to brothers and sisters. It can be a word of exhortation, consolation, salvation, but always for edification and under the guidance of the Holy Spirit through the Word of God. Prophecies are not to be despised, for they are from God. Likewise, we must respect the one who brings the prophetic word, as a vessel useful to the Master.

but test everything; hold fast what is good. (5:21)

For the Thessalonians, the standards for testing all things, especially prophecy, were found in the Old Testament and Paul's instructions. As for us, we are privileged to possess the entire Word of God. Especially with regard to prophecies about future events, many so-called prophets and commentators of prophecy are manifesting themselves today. We need to be vigilant, to be like those noble Bereans who "received the word with all eagerness, examining the Scriptures daily to see if these things were so" (Acts 17:11). For our benefit, we must discern and hold on to those things which are good.

Abstain from every form of evil. (5:22)

To the young believers of Thessalonica, Paul addresses himself in a categorical way. There is no question of examining the different forms evil can take. If prophecies are to be analyzed and if we are to retain what is good, evil in all its forms must be rejected. Let us be "wise as to what is good, and innocent as to what is evil" (Rom. 16:19). This is our safeguard.

57

c. Recommendations to God's grace and final exhortations (5:23-28)

Now may the God of peace himself sanctify you completely, and may your whole spirit and soul and body be kept blameless at the coming of our Lord Jesus Christ. (5:23)

The topic of holiness, like the topics of encouragement and the coming of the Lord, is an important theme in Paul's letter: holiness in service in chapter 2 (v. 10), holiness in affection in chapter 3 (v. 11-13), and holiness in Christian walk in chapter 4 (v. 1-8). Alone, we are powerless to achieve holiness in our lives, to separate ourselves from this world in order to consecrate ourselves to Christ and His interests. We must rely on God who can sanctify us completely, so that we will be kept blameless until the return of the Lord. Our whole person must be kept blameless: our spirit, which encompasses our intellectual capacities, our soul, which is the seat of our feelings and affections, and our physical being.

He who calls you is faithful; he will surely do it. (5:24)

God, the God of peace, gave His peace to our consciences when we believed in His Son and His work on the cross of Calvary. His peace now keeps our hearts and minds in Christ Jesus (Phil. 4:7). In spite of our failings, our God is faithful to carry out His plans for us, especially His plan to sanctify us completely. He will not fail to complete what He has set out to do for us.

Brothers, pray for us. (5:25)

Since we have the privilege of being brothers and sisters in the Lord, it is our responsibility to pray for each other, and also for the servants of the Lord. Paul, Silvanus, and Timothy mentioned the Thessalonians in their prayers (1:2). Now they, in turn, were asking for the prayers of the saints.

Greet all the brothers with a holy kiss. (5:26)

The greetings of Paul and his companions are for all the brothers. They are expressed warmly with a holy kiss. See also Rom. 16:16, 1 Cor. 16:20. 2 Cor. 13:12, 1 Pet. 5:14.

I put you under oath before the Lord to have this letter read to all the [holy] brothers. (5:27)

Paul's letter communicated the word of the Lord. It was fitting, therefore, that this letter should be read to all the holy brothers and sisters, i.e., those set apart for the Lord. It is to the advantage of all of us, even today, to read and listen carefully to the Word of God.

The grace of our Lord Jesus Christ be with you. (5:28)

This final greeting is characteristic of all the letters of the apostle Paul. We find in it the mention of grace, that great subject of joy for our hearts. Just as in His time on earth, the Lord still uses grace towards us now in glory.

తించం

The Lord Jesus Christ desires that each one of us, brother or sister, should enjoy this grace today and until He returns. Let us draw it abundantly from Him through all our circumstances so that we may be encouraged in our journey here below before we meet Him.

PAUL'S SECOND LETTER TO THE THESSALONIANS

INTRODUCTION

In his first letter, the apostle Paul had given words of encouragement to the young believers in Thessalonica who were saddened by the death of some among them. These young believers thought that their beloved ones asleep in the Lord would be absent when the Lord Jesus would manifest Himself to the world. For the inspired writer, this was the opportunity to present the precious truths of the First Epistle to the Thessalonians about the coming of the Lord for His people. At this coming, the believers who have died will first be resurrected and then we, the living who remain on the earth, will be caught up with them to meet the Lord in the air. Later, we will all return with Him to be manifested to the world in glory in His day.

In his first letter, Paul had encouraged the Thessalonians, until then in ignorance of the subject of dead believers, the dead in Christ. In this second letter, he addresses the same Thessalonians who were upset and troubled by the persecutions and trials which they, the living believers, had to endure. Some people, by word and letter, had even seduced the young Christian church by proclaiming that the day of the Lord had come. These false teachings were not without having a negative effect on this local church: many were discouraged. More seriously, others were walking in a disorderly manner: not working and meddling in everything.

This Second Epistle of Paul to the Thessalonians is also a letter of encouragement to the believers of all times. Our encouragement comes, first of all, from the Lord Jesus and God the Father: we have been loved and have received eternal comfort (or: encouragement; *paraklesis*, in Greek) and good hope through grace (2:16). During our stay here on earth, our weak hearts are comforted (or: encouraged) and we are established (or: strengthened) by the Father and the Son in our Christian walk (2:17). In a special way, the letter blames the brothers who walked in disorder by refusing to work quietly and earn their own living (literally, in Greek: eat their own bread) (3:12).

This letter of the apostle is also very instructive because of the details it gives us about the prophetic events that will take place between the rapture of believers and the day of the Lord's manifestation to the world. The man of sin, the Antichrist, will reveal himself during this period and, under the impulse of Satan, stand against God and seek to take His place. But the Lord Jesus will destroy him through the appearance of His coming (2 Thes. 2:8). We do well to be attentive to this prophetic word, for it produces in us an ever-growing desire to see the One whom we love and wait for, the Lord Jesus as the Morning Star (2 Pet. 1:19).

In order to facilitate the study of this letter verse by verse, we will adopt the following five major sections: the revelation of the Lord Jesus, the appearance of His coming, the encouragement by the Father and the Son, the encouragement to walk in an orderly manner, and the final greetings.

We are confident that the reading of the verses of God's Word and the commentaries that accompany them will be an encouragement to wait earnestly for the Lord Jesus from heaven. May the Morning Star already begin to rise in our hearts during this time of vigil (2 Pet. 1:19)!

I

THE REVELATION OF
THE LORD JESUS

Chapter 1

In his letters to churches and individuals, the apostle Paul sends greetings and thanksgiving to God. The Second Epistle to the Thessalonians is no exception. However, we will see in the first section of our comments, corresponding to the first chapter of this epistle, that Paul soon came to the main reason that prompted him to write this letter: the persecutions and afflictions that the Thessalonians had to endure (v. 4). Already in verse 5, he explains to them that if they suffer, it is so that they may be considered worthy of the kingdom of God. Their sufferings, moreover, are only for a time, for there is relief to come at the revelation of the Lord Jesus Christ (v. 7). For unbelievers, vengeance and eternal destruction will mark that same day (vv. 8-9). Meanwhile, the apostle prayed that the believers in Thessalonica would be judged worthy of God's calling (vv. 11-12).

a. *Greetings (1:1, 2)*

Paul, Silvanus, and Timothy, To the church of the Thessalonians in God our Father and the Lord Jesus Christ: (1:1)

65

At the beginning of this second letter to the Thessalonians, Paul associates to himself the same two brothers, Silvanus and Timothy, as in the first letter. Paul and his companions address all the Christians of Thessalonica, who then formed the church, or assembly, of this city in Greece. These things, like every scripture of the Word of God, are also written for our spiritual instruction and growth, that we may be complete and equipped for every good work (2 Tim. 3: 16, 17).

Again, the church in Thessalonica is characterized as being "in God our Father"—a precious relationship based on the work of the Lord Jesus on the cross. The Risen Lord could say, "I am ascending to my Father and your Father, to my God and your God" (John 20:17). In the first letter, Paul addresses the church in God *the* Father; in the second letter, he addresses the church in God *our* Father. The apostle now seems to desire for these young believers a greater realization of the close relationship that unites them to the God and Father of our Lord Jesus Christ. Our fellowship is also "in the Lord Jesus Christ" (1 Cor. 1:9) who has revealed to us his God and Father. For us, the Lord is the One who has authority over our individual lives and over local churches.

Grace to you and peace from God our Father and the Lord Jesus Christ. (1:2)

Paul is the spokesman of divine persons in greeting the church of Thessalonica: he is doing so on behalf of God the Father and the Lord Jesus Christ. According to the best manuscripts available to translators, the first epistle does not mention the source of the greetings. It is simply written "Grace and peace to you." This second epistle of the apostle Paul was meant to be a very special source of encouragement, given the sufferings of these young believers. From the outset, the apostle makes them aware of the interest that God the Father and the Lord Jesus Christ have in them.

We have noticed in the previous comments on the first epistle that the expression "Grace and peace" is used in all Paul's letters. In this second letter, Paul twice expresses his obligation to give thanks for his brothers (1:3 and 2:13). We learn the origin of grace: it is from God and from the Lord Jesus Christ (1:12); it is also the means by which God has given us eternal comfort and good hope (2:16). As for peace, it is the Lord of peace Himself who gives it to us always and in every way (3:16).

b. *Reasons to give thanks (1:3-5)*

We ought always to give thanks to God for you, brothers, as is right, because your faith is growing abundantly, and the love of every one of you for one another is increasing. (1:3)

Paul likes to give thanks to God for the churches (see in addition to our verse: Rom. 1. 8, 1 Cor. 1. 4, Eph. 1. 16, Phil. 1. 3, Col. 1. 3, 1 Thes. 1. 2). He refrained from addressing the believers in Corinth in this manner in his second letter to them, because he wanted them first to reaffirm their love for the brother who had been disciplined in that church. As for the Galatians who were placing themselves under the law, Paul wanted to see them, first of all, freed from the yoke of bondage, in order to enjoy the freedom in which Christ has placed us. But it was only in the case of the Thessalonians that Paul could say that he was always bound to give thanks. These thanksgivings added to the fragrance of the prayers the apostle always said for them (1:11).

Therefore we ourselves boast about you in the churches of God for your steadfastness and faith in all your persecutions and in the afflictions that you are enduring. (1:4)

In the first letter, Paul wrote to the Thessalonians, telling them that they were his hope, his joy, his crown of boasting before the Lord (1 Thes. 2:19). In our verse, Paul boasts about them in the churches of God. He would certainly have liked to boast about their patience of hope, as in the first epistle (1:3); but he discerned behind the outwardly visible patience that their hope was wavering. The Enemy had succeeded in opening a breach by overburdening them with various sufferings, which made the prospect of the Lord Jesus' appearance to take them to Himself secondary in their consideration. In spite of this weakness regarding hope, which is the helmet of the Christian believer, faith and love still acted as a breastplate (1 Thes. 5:8).

Paul himself had experienced persecution: the Jews had driven him out more than once through persecution (Acts 13:50 and 1 Thes. 2:15). He was therefore well able to understand the persecutions endured by these young believers and to boast in them, for they testified to their godliness. As for the afflictions, they overwhelm the spirit like a burden. From the beginning of their Christian life, those of Thessalonica had received the Word accompanied by much affliction, but with the joy of the Holy Spirit (1 Thes. 1:6). To those who suffer for the Lord, who experience tribulation in this world, He tells them to take heart, for He has overcome the world (John 16:33).

This is evidence of the righteous judgment of God, that you may be considered worthy of the kingdom of God, for which you are also suffering— (1:5)

Human beings have a natural aversion to the idea of suffering. They denounce suffering and do their best to avert it, or at least to alleviate it, but without realizing that it is a consequence of the introduction of sin into the world. The Christian, on the other hand, is called to suffer for the kingdom of God. He knows that it is through many afflictions—it is the same word in Greek as "tribulations"—that he or she must enter the kingdom of God (Acts 14:22).

This verse 5 does not mean that we must suffer to be made worthy of the kingdom of God. Rather, we can think of these sufferings as a kind of a seal to testify that they were worthy of the kingdom. The Lord had said that "whoever does not take his cross and follow me is not worthy of me" (Matt. 10:38). At the beginning of the Christian testimony, therefore, Peter and the other apostles were "rejoicing that they were counted worthy to suffer dishonor for the name" of Christ (Acts 5:41).

This same Peter was qualified to encourage the Jews of the dispersion who were experiencing various sufferings; he does this in his first epistle. He writes firstly about the sufferings for a little while which constitute the test of faith, but which will produce praise and glory and honor in the revelation of Jesus Christ (1:6, 7). Secondly, he tells us that it is a gracious thing for one who, mindful of God, bears afflictions, suffering unjustly (2:19). Thirdly, he calls blessed those who suffer for the sake of righteousness (3:14). Fourthly, he also calls blessed those who are insulted for the name of Christ, who share in Christ's sufferings (4:13, 14). Finally, he declares that those who suffer trials arising from the opposition of the devil will be restored, confirmed, strengthened, and established by the God of all grace (5:8-10).

When God pronounces His judgment, it will be evident to all that it is a just judgment. Unbelievers will be punished for the persecutions and tribulations with which they have afflicted the saints (2 Thes. 1:6). At the time of this judgment, when the Lord Jesus will be revealed to the world, the saints will enjoy relief.

c. *The Revelation of the Lord Jesus (1:6-10)*

since indeed God considers it just to repay with affliction those who afflict you,

The unbeliever might challenge the justice of a God who is love and yet renders tribulation to one who is guilty of inflicting it on a believer. However, he will have to learn at the Lord's revelation that not only is the believer of a great price in the eyes of God, but that what is inflicted on the believer is personally inflicted on Christ. To

Paul, who persecuted Christians before his conversion, the Lord had said, "Saul, Saul, why are you persecuting me?" (Acts 9:4).

Vengeance on all unbelievers will result in the punishment of eternal destruction away from the presence of the Lord. God is also the One "that rewards those who seek him." (Heb. 11:6). He will give relief to those who have suffered tribulation. We rightly like to talk about God's love for human beings. However, this love is not exercised at the expense of justice, which is one of the characteristics of the divine nature, just as love is.

and to grant relief [or rest] to you who are afflicted as well as to us, when the Lord Jesus is revealed from heaven with his mighty angels (1:7)

The Lord Jesus is the One who gives rest to lost sinners, bent under the weight of their misery (Matt. 11:28); this is the rest of the conscience. There is also rest for the soul of believers weary in the way: it is by taking the yoke of the Lord and learning from Him that we find rest for our souls (Matt. 11:29). Our verse mentions relief (also translated "rest"); this rest is similar to the rest referred to in the book of Hebrews: "there remains a Sabbath rest for the people of God" (Heb. 4:9). This Sabbath rest corresponds to the millennial reign of Christ which will follow His revelation from heaven. "For the Lord will have compassion on Jacob and will again choose Israel, and will set them [or: give them rest] in their own land, and sojourners will join them and will attach themselves to the house of Jacob [...] The whole earth is at rest and quiet; they break forth into singing." (Isaiah 14:1, 7).

As for us, in heaven with our Lord, we will enjoy the eternal rest into which He entered after His victory over the Enemy on the cross. But a serious warning is given to those who now despise such a great salvation; they will be thrown into the lake of fire: "The smoke of their torment goes up forever and ever, and they have no rest, day or night..." (Rev. 14:11). Their fate will resemble that of the multitudes who followed the Beast.

Believers will enter into rest when they go to meet Christ at the rapture of the Church. Therefore, they will already enjoy rest at the Lord's subsequent revelation to the world. In chapter 2 of the epistle, we will discuss the revelation of the Antichrist (the man of lawlessness, the son of destruction), the one who presents himself as God. But in our verse, the believer rejoices to hear about the revelation of his Lord first. In the study of prophecy, He must occupy the first place, otherwise this study risks degenerating into a futile intellectual exercise. It is from heaven that the Lord Jesus will be revealed: He will come in the same way that the apostles saw Him go to heaven (Acts 1:11). The angels will be the instruments of His power in the judgment of the nations, before His kingdom is established (e.g.: Rev. 9:15.)

in flaming fire, inflicting vengeance on those who do not know God and on those who do not obey the gospel of our Lord Jesus. (1:8)

Vengeance (or retribution) is an aspect of the manifestation of divine justice at the revelation of the Lord Jesus from heaven. The Lord, through the voice of the prophet Isaiah, said to Zion concerning her future restoration: "Behold, your God will come with vengeance, with the recompense of God. He will come and save you." (Isaiah 35:4). The Lord with His heavenly armies will take vengeance on unbelievers; God will reward the believer by giving him relief from his tribulation

The Greek word for vengeance could be translated literally as "that which proceeds from righteousness." Vengeance is the extension, the manifestation of divine justice. Believers must not take revenge: "Beloved, never avenge yourselves" (Rom. 12:19). This same verse, as well as Heb. 10:30, reminds us of the divine prerogative: "Vengeance is mine; I will repay, says the Lord." Thus the author of the Hebrews quotes Deuteronomy 32:35: "Vengeance is mine, and recompense, for the time when their foot shall slip."

The Lord can avenge a brother who transgresses and wrongs his brother (1 Thes. 4:6). Here, the Lord's vengeance is exercised against those who do not know God—in the time of the apostle, those of the Gentiles who lived in the passion of lust (1 Thes. 4:5); it is also exercised against those who do not obey the Gospel—still at that time, the Jews who prevented the preaching of salvation to the Gentiles (1 Thes. 2:16). It can be suggested that today those who do not know God are all those who refuse such a great salvation; those who do not obey the gospel include those who have only the name of Christian and who hold to a gospel different from the gospel of grace of our Lord Jesus Christ (see, for example, Gal. 1:8, 9).

They will suffer the punishment of eternal destruction, away from the presence of the Lord and from the glory of his might, (1:9)

This is the Lord's vengeance on those who do not know God and those who do not obey the gospel: the punishment of eternal perdition (or: ruin, destruction). The punishment is the execution of God's just sentence against all ungodliness and unrighteousness of men who are worthy of death. We can read Rom. 1:18-32 on this subject. This punishment is not a death that merely ends life. It is eternal perdition, which rules out annihilation. Jude 7 tells us of a punishment of eternal fire. How solemn is this thought of an eternity away from God, of eternal torments "into hell, where their worm does not die and the fire is not quenched" (Mark 9:48). Whoever rejects God's salvation will not be able to escape from this eternity of destruction. Already on earth foolish and pernicious desires can plunge men into ruin and perdition (1 Tim. 6:9); this earthly punishment will lead to eternal perdition. The destruction under the reign of the Antichrist (the man of lawlessness, the son of destruction) will be sudden like the pain that comes upon a pregnant woman, and unexpected like the coming of a thief in the night; sinners who have not repented will not escape (1 Thes. 5:2, 3).

The presence of the Lord (literally: His face) and the glory of His power will be enough to bring the punishment of eternal destruction. We read that the appearance of Jesus was marred beyond human semblance (Isaiah 52:14). There were those who spit in His face, and He did not resist when He was struck (Matt. 26:67). This is the same Man of Sorrows of old whose face of glory will be seen in the future. Not only will opponents retreat and fall to the ground before Him as they did in the garden of Gethsemane (Jn. 18:6), but they will also receive the punishment of their disbelief.

when he comes on that day to be glorified in his saints, and to be marveled at among all who have believed, because our testimony to you was believed. (1:10)

Verses 8 and 9 have given us a picture of the negative aspect of the Lord's Day. Vengeance and eternal destruction will be inflicted on those who do not know God and those who do not obey the gospel of our Lord Jesus Christ. Verse 10 presents the positive aspect of the Lord's Day, when He will be glorified and admired. It is the day of the revelation of the Lord Jesus from heaven (v. 7). Seducers upset the Thessalonians by leading them to believe that "the day of the Lord (had) come" (2:2). However, the fact that the Lord had not taken vengeance on His enemies and had not manifested Himself in those who believed showed the falsity of such teachings spread by these deceivers.

The Thessalonians were among those who had believed. The Lord Jesus will therefore be glorified in them also at His coming. We read elsewhere that if we suffer with the Lord—this was the situation of the Thessalonians—we will also be glorified with Him (Rom. 8:17). This promise is precious for our hearts, but our verse offers something even more wonderful. The world will witness the glory of Christ manifested in His saints. The saints will perfectly reflect the glory of Christ, for they themselves will contemplate His glory face to face and will be transformed into the same image from glory to glory (2 Cor. 3:18). At present, this moral transformation takes place in the believer by contemplating the Lord by faith; then it will be by seeing Him in all His majesty. The Lord Jesus will be able to say: "This is the fruit of the toilsome labor of my soul!" (see Isaiah 53:11). What a joy for His heart! The Lord will be admired in all of us who have believed, not by virtue of anything of ourselves worthy of praise, but by virtue of the results of the glorious and powerful work of God in us. What a spectacle for angels and men to see the fruit of God's grace in each one of the redeemed!

d. *Worthy of the calling (1:11, 12)*

To this end we always pray for you, that our God may make [count] you worthy of his calling and may fulfill every resolve for good [all the good pleasure of his goodness] and every work of faith by his power, (1:11).

Paul and his companions did not pray for the Thessalonians to be made worthy of God's calling: having believed, they were already worthy. They prayed that they would be counted (or judged) worthy of this calling. This is a very important distinction. The illustration of the prodigal son in Luke 15 sheds more light on this doctrinal point. After his troubles in the far country and having returned to himself after a work of repentance, the son says to his father: "Father, I have sinned against heaven and before you. I am no longer worthy *to be called* your son" (Luke 15:21). He does not say, "I am no longer worthy *to be* your son." He could not lose the dignity of being a son, for it belonged to him by virtue of his relationship with his father from birth; but he could rightly consider himself unworthy of this appellation.

It is the same for us. Our dignity is inherent in the fact that we are "all sons of God, through faith in Christ Jesus" (Gal. 3:26). Our Christian walk, however, must be consistent with our calling. On the one hand, God's words cannot change: "the gifts and the calling of God call are irrevocable" (Rom. 11:29). On the other hand, our responsibility is to "walk in a manner worthy of the calling to which (we) have been called" (Eph. 4:1) and to "be all the more diligent to confirm (our) calling and election" (2 Pet. 1:10).

Paul and his friends always prayed also that God would fulfill His good pleasure in them. God's delight was in the Beloved before His human manifestation (Proverbs 8:30), as well as during His life on earth (e.g., Isaiah 42:1; Matt. 12:18; 2 Pet. 1:17). What is the reason for this? Because the Son always did the things that were pleasing to the Father (John 8:29). But as far as we are concerned, God must fulfill in us the good pleasure of His goodness, i.e., that which corresponds to His very nature. He must also produce the work of faith. Paul had witnessed this in Thessalonica (1 Thes. 1:3). Here he can pray for God to accomplish it in power, for he knew that the difficult circumstances of the Thessalonians, their persecutions and afflictions (or tribulations), were a favorable ground for the unfolding of the Lord's power. Paul had experienced personally and in a very special way that the power of the Lord is fulfilled in weakness. He therefore was content with his weaknesses, so that the power of Christ might rest upon him (2 Cor. 12:7-10).

so that the name of our Lord Jesus may be glorified in you, and you in him, according to the grace of our God and the Lord Jesus Christ. (1:12)

Fully satisfied with the work done by His Son to glorify Him on earth, the Father now glorifies the Son in heaven with the glory which He had with Him before the foundation of the world. He has also exalted the Man Christ Jesus and has given Him the name above every name: see John 17:1-5 and Phil. 2:9. If the person of the Lord

Jesus is glorified by the Father in the heavenly sphere, the heart of God also desires that His name be glorified on earth in believers.

God's work in us is always aimed at the glory of Christ. Among the Thessalonians, this work was particularly connected with suffering for the kingdom of God. The Lord was glorified in them in anticipation of the day when they would be glorified in Him. Only the grace of God and the Lord Jesus Christ can work in us so that Christ may be glorified in our lives today and we may be glorified in Him when he returns.

The lesson we learn from these first verses of the epistle is that, despite difficult personal circumstances, perhaps persecutions and trials as in the case of the Thessalonians, the Lord must be glorified in our lives. May the prospect of resting soon with our Beloved encourage us to persevere in our Christian journey to heaven!

II

THE APPEARANCE OF THE COMING OF THE LORD JESUS

Chapter 2, verses 1-12

The second chapter of the epistle continues the theme begun in the first epistle: the revelation of the Lord Jesus in His day. The Thessalonians had been led to believe that the day of the Lord had come. The apostle's answer to these false teachings is very simple: it could not be so, because the gathering of the believers to the Lord had not happened. Moreover, before that day, apostasy will reach its full development and the man of sin will be revealed. The apostle gives details of the revelation of the lawless one which will be followed by the judgment of unbelievers. Already today, we are witnessing signs of the operation of this mystery of wickedness: the increasingly manifest attachment to seductive spirits and demons, as well as widespread selfishness. These signs are precursors of the full manifestation of wickedness when the Antichrist will appear in a future day and exalt himself.

a. *The Day of the Lord (2:1-4)*

Now concerning the coming of our Lord Jesus Christ and our being gathered together to him, we ask you, brothers, (2. 1)

In response to the concerns of the Thessalonians about whether the day of the Lord had come, Paul first refers to the promise of the coming of the Lord. Their tribulations and persecutions were not to make them forget that the coming of the Lord will be in two stages. In the first place, the Lord will come to take His own people: this is the blessed hope, an event that will take place without the world's knowledge. The dead in Christ will be raised, and the living who will remain on earth will be caught up together in the clouds to meet the Lord in the air (1 Thes. 4:15-18). Obviously, this event had not happened. Secondly, the Lord will return a little later, i.e.: in His day, to appear in glory with His people: every eye will see Him (Rev. 1:7). But this day of the Lord will not be brought without great tribulation on the inhabited earth (see Matt. 24:1-31).

Paul then speaks of our gathering to the Lord, i.e., the coming of the Lord specifically to take us to be with Himself. This event must necessarily precede our return with the Lord in order to establish His reign. Thus, the apostle refutes these "new" teachings contrary to those he had taught them, using the argument that the day of the Lord could not be here, since the gathering to the Lord was yet future.

The coming of the Lord is often confused with the day of the Lord. The expression the coming of the Lord, which is translated from the Greek word *parousia*, literally means to be by the side. This coming of the Lord includes His coming for His saints and His presence with them until His revelation and manifestation to the world. As for the expression gathering together with the Lord, we find this word—*episunagogê*, in Greek—elsewhere only in the Epistle to the Hebrews in chapter 10, verse 25, where we are exhorted not to abandon our gathering around the Lord. These two gatherings are of equal value in the eyes of the Lord. Should they not be for each one of the Lord's redeemed? Let us consider it a precious privilege to have the Lord in the midst of those who gather in His name (Matt. 18:20), just as His presence will be when we go to meet Him at the rapture!

not to be quickly shaken in mind or alarmed, either by a spirit or a spoken word, or a letter seeming to be from us, to the effect that the day of the Lord has come. (2:2)

Because they were experiencing persecution and tribulation, the Thessalonians were convinced that the day of the Lord was here. To demonstrate that it was not so, the apostle makes the main argument that the gathering of the believers to the Lord had to happen first. Other arguments will be advanced in the following verses. However, the first evidence was already sufficient to put an end to their fears. These fears were aroused by the false teachings of seducers claiming to have the mind of God, and therefore to be inspired. A letter was even written, supposedly by Paul, to frighten the Thessalonians. Paul denies being its author. The genuineness of his letters could be recognized by the fact that he wrote the greeting with his own hand at the end of each letter (see 3:17).

Obviously, the Thessalonians had allowed themselves to be quickly shaken in mind or alarmed in their conviction that the Lord should first gather them to Himself before His day. It has been said that the Thessalonians, in their difficult circumstances, resembled a ship whose moorings had been loosened by the storm. The Lord uses the same Greek word for "to be alarmed" in Matt. 24:6 and Mark 13:7 when He warns the apostles—a picture of the faithful Jewish residue of the end—not to be alarmed by false christs, wars, and rumors of war, because the end will not be yet at hand. Paul, like his Master, does not want the believers in Thessalonica to be troubled by those who sought to deceive them, nor by the painful circumstances they were going through.

Two other events must precede the day of the Lord: the general apostasy and the revelation of the man of sin.

Let no one deceive you in any way. For that day will not come, unless the rebellion [or: the apostasy] comes first, and the man of lawlessness is revealed, the son of destruction, (2:3)

Satan is the deceiver par excellence, but the Thessalonians had to be especially warned against his agents. The Word mentions deception for the first time when Eve, in the garden, said to the Lord God that the serpent deceived her and she ate the fruit of the forbidden tree (Genesis 3:13). This was Satan's first victory. The last mention of deception is also related to the Enemy of our souls: but at that time Satan will be bound for a thousand years and thrown into the abyss that he should not any more deceive the nations during the reign of Christ (Rev. 20:1-3).

Deception accompanies apostasy, this abandonment of faith and Christian life. Apostasy is the complete rejection of the Word of God, and the Gospel of salvation by grace in particular. Paul writes to Timothy that we are witnessing a partial turning away from the faith: "The Spirit expressly says that in later times some will depart from the faith by devoting themselves to deceitful spirits and teachings of demons" (1 Tim. 4:1). We are witnessing today such signs of the final apostasy foreshadowing the revelation of the man of sin who is none other than the Antichrist.

We know what character and the end of this man of sin will be even before he is manifested, for he is the son of destruction, i.e.: the man who brings destruction and the man whose end is destruction. The Lord Jesus also called Judas Iscariot, the one who was to betray Him, the son of destruction (John 17:12). Already we recognize many deceivers and antichrists in those who do not confess the coming of Jesus Christ in the flesh (2 John 7). But the ultimate Antichrist has not yet been manifested. When he appears, it is only gradually that he will reveal his true intentions.

who opposes and exalts himself against every so-called god or object of worship, so that he takes his seat in the temple of God, proclaiming himself to be God. (2:4)

The man of sin, the son of destruction, corresponds to the one whom the apostle John calls the Antichrist. The Antichrist attacks both the promise of Judaism by denying that Jesus is the Christ (1 John 2:22) and that He came in the flesh (1 John 4:3, 2 John 7), as well as the foundation of Christianity by denying the Father and the Son (1 John 2:22). Peter had said of Jesus that He was the Christ (Matt. 16:16): this was the recognition of a truth proper to Judaism. The Lord had made the Father known (John 14:7-9): this is a revelation proper to Christianity.

The Antichrist is not only the one who presents himself in the place of Christ, but also the one who opposes Christ. Daniel 11 teaches us that he is that king who "shall do as he wills. He shall exalt himself and magnify himself above every god, and shall speak astonishing things against the God of gods. He shall prosper till the indignation is accomplished" (v. 36). Here, the Antichrist opposes and rises up against everything that has to do with God.

We also recognize the Antichrist in this "other Beast rising out of the earth. It had two horns like a lamb and it spoke like a dragon" (Rev. 13:11). The earth here symbolizes the Judaic system. The first Beast (Rev. 13:1-10) rises from the sea, a figure of the nations. The second, or other Beast, whose religious dominion will be exercised from Jerusalem, will seek to take the place of the Lord Jesus, the true Lamb of God; but, speaking like a dragon, his voice betrays the one who keeps him in place and allows him to exercise the power of the first Beast and great miracles: it is none other than the dragon, that ancient serpent, who is the devil and Satan (Rev. 20:2).

The Antichrist will push his claims to the point of sitting in the temple of God. This is "the abomination of desolation spoken of by the prophet Daniel, standing in the holy place" (Matt. 24:15; see Daniel 12:11). (Note that an earlier fulfillment of the desolation of Daniel 11:31 has already taken place: it is the desecration of the temple of Jerusalem by Antiochus Epiphanes before the Christian era). In addition to usurping the place of God, the Antichrist will present himself as God. However, he remains a man with his weaknesses and inconsistencies: he himself will honor a god, the god of fortresses (a god of his own invention), and promote this worship (Daniel 11:37, 38).

b. *The mystery of iniquity (2:5-7)*

Do you not remember that when I was still with you I told you these things? (2:5)

During his brief stay in Thessalonica to preach the gospel, Paul had instructed the Thessalonians in many things. He had spoken to them about the Lord: His sufferings, His death, His resurrection. He had shown them that He was Christ (Acts 17:1-3). He had told them in advance that they would have to undergo tribulation, as it had happened, and he had taught them about the day of the Lord (1 Thes. 3: 3, 4; 5: 1-5). Here, we learn that he also instructed them about the events preceding this day, such as those related to the revelation of the Antichrist.

If the Thessalonians had remembered the apostle's teachings, they would not have been quickly upset and troubled by those who claimed that the Lord's Day had come. On the one hand, this brings out the importance of paying attention not only to the written Word, but also to the Word presented in a meeting of a prophetic character (according to 1 Cor. 14). On the other hand, every servant of the Lord must make every effort to ensure that souls always remember the things that are of God, even if these things seem to be well known and even if the listeners seem to be established in the present truth (2 Pet. 1:12). Moreover, the true teacher of the Word has the heart of a shepherd: he desires to ensure that his listeners will remember his teachings after his departure (2 Pet. 1:15).

And you know what is restraining him now so that he may be revealed in his time. (2:6)

We have noticed that the day of the Lord will not come before the general apostasy and the revelation of the man of sin. In this verse, the apostle instructs the Thessalonians concerning the fact that this revelation of the Antichrist cannot take place now, for there is that which restrains (our v. 6) and the One who restrains (v. 7). It has been suggested that what holds back evil corresponds to the governments of men whose authority comes from God, or the presence of the Church on earth. Until it is gathered to the Lord, the Church, by its presence on earth, is a restraint to the overflow of evil and prevents the revelation of the lawless one. As long as the believers are on the earth and have not been raptured, the flood of iniquity will be held back.

Now, even though the Lord's day must be preceded by the apostasy and revelation of the Antichrist, and this revelation cannot take place before our gathering to the Lord, no event must necessarily precede the Lord's coming for His people. The Lord's promise remains as real and precious as ever: "I am coming soon!" (Rev. 22:7, 12, 20). The redeemed believer awaits his Lord's return at any time.

For the mystery of lawlessness is already at work. Only he who now restrains it will do so until he is out of the way. (2:7)

The mysteries of God's Word are not defined as incomprehensible truths that we must believe. They are truths that were once obscure, but are now revealed. There are the mysteries of the kingdom of God (Luke 8:10), the partial hardening of Israel (Rom. 11:25), Christ and the Church (Eph. 5:32), the gospel (Eph. 6:19), and godliness (1 Tim. 3:16). The mystery of lawlessness corresponds to that wickedness of man which knows no restraint and which will reach its full development by manifesting itself thoroughly in the person of the Antichrist.

In the 19th century, it was written that "Christianity now speaks much more of morality and humanitarian works than of the person of Christ and increasingly tends to do without a revealed religion". What can be said now of the ever-increasing number of followers of humanist movements who claim to be gods, some of whom even seek to rely on verses of the Word while ignoring the contexts of these verses? The divine answer to this claim is: "The gods who did not make heaven and earth, these shall perish from the earth and from under the heavens" (Jeremiah 10:11).

The Holy Spirit who dwells in the Church (Eph. 2:22) holds back a greater outpouring of iniquity; He restrains that energy of evil which has its source in Satan. He will do this until He is out of the way, i.e., until the Church, which is God's temple, is caught up in the clouds to meet the Lord in the air and He, the Holy Spirit, is no longer present on earth in that temple (see 1 Cor. 3:16-17). The departure of the Holy Spirit and the Church, at the time of the rapture, will leave the field free for the revelation of the lawless one. However, the expression "until he is out of the way" leaves room for the possibility of a certain lapse of time between the departure of the Holy Spirit (and the rapture of believers) and this revelation of the lawless one.

c. *The Revelation of the lawless one (2:8-10)*

And then the lawless one will be revealed, whom the Lord Jesus will kill with the breath of his mouth and bring to nothing by the appearance of his coming. (2:8)

Iniquity will find its full manifestation in the Antichrist, the lawless one in person. Satan will give him his power. As we have seen, the Antichrist will act according to his own will and stand against God.

He will be the opposite of what the Lord has been on earth: gentle and lowly in heart (Matt. 11. 29), dependent on His Father and submitted to Him.

The overflow of wickedness will be such that the Lord Himself will intervene in judgment. We know the fate of the Antichrist: The Lord will destroy and annihilate him by His appearance when He comes with His saints to judge the earth and establish His reign of peace. How remarkable will be the effect produced by the Lord's presence! The Antichrist (the false prophet) will be captured together with the first Beast (who will join forces with the kings of the earth and their armies gathered to fight against the Lord). This Beast and the false prophet will both be thrown alive into the lake of fire that burns with sulfur. This is what we read in the Book of Revelation (19:19-21).

The coming of the lawless one is by the activity of Satan with all power and false signs and wonders, (2:9)

Although the mystery of lawlessness is already at work according to Satan's evil activity, the coming of the Antichrist is future. This coming will also be according to the activity—*energeia*, in Greek—of Satan, who will be free to act in a world where the presence and activity of the Holy Spirit will be absent. Satan, from whom the power of the Antichrist actually emanates, will suffer a fate similar to that of the Antichrist. An angel will seize this enemy defeated by Christ at the cross, bind him for a thousand years, and cast him into the abyss. At the end of the thousand years, he will be released for a little while to lead the nations astray, and then he will be thrown into the lake of fire that burns with sulfur where the two Beasts (referred to, in this passage, as the Beast and the false prophet) will already be. These events are found in Rev. 19:17 to 20:10.

Satan's energy deployed by the Antichrist will be manifested in all power, false signs and wonders (or: signs and lying wonders) by which he will deceive as many people as possible: those who will receive the mark of the Beast and will worship its image (Rev. 19:20). These miracles, false signs and wonders correspond to the character of the devil: he is a liar and the father of lies (John 8:44).

Although his coming is according to the operation of Satan, the Antichrist will come in his own name and will be received by the world, as prophetically announced by the Lord Jesus (John 5:43). The Lord had come in the name of His Father; He was that man approved of God among the Jews by the miracles, wonders and signs which He performed among them (Acts 2:22). It has been said that "the Lord by His miracles shows the grace and power of God; the Evil One will work them to exalt himself in his boundless pride and to be worshiped." What a contrast between the Savior, gentle and lowly in heart, and this proud man of sin!

and with all wicked deception for those who are perishing, because they refused to love the truth and so be saved. (2:10)

The Lord rebukes the king of Tyre, a type of Satan, for the multitude of his iniquities and the unrighteousness of his trade (Ezekiel 28:18). This unrighteousness truly characterizes the seductive influence that the Antichrist, the instrument of Satan, will exert on those who dwell on the earth. At present, many who apostatized from the faith attach themselves to deceitful spirits and demonic teachings (1 Tim. 4:1). How much more effective will this seduction be when the Spirit is out of the way!

If we are saved by grace, which is the gift of God (Eph. 2:8), the responsibility of those who perish falls entirely on themselves. They did not receive the love of the truth, but had pleasure in unrighteousness (v. 12 below). Rather than receiving the salvation of their souls by believing in the Lord, who has manifested grace and truth (John 1:17), who is the truth (John 14:6), and who has given His Father's word, which is the truth (John 17:17), men prefer and will prefer unrighteousness. Unrighteousness manifests itself in the last days through selfishness, greed, boasting, and other sins; people will be lovers of self, money, and pleasure rather than lovers of God (2 Tim. 3:1-5).

d. *The judgment of the unbelievers (2:11, 12)*

Therefore God sends them a strong delusion, so that they may believe what is false, (2:11)

The love of truth can save a sinful man. But under the dominion of the Beast and the Antichrist, those who refuse this love will receive from God Himself a strong delusion, i.e., an energy or power of error. God had hardened the heart of Pharaoh who refused to let His people go (Exodus 10:1). He gave up unrighteous individuals to a debased mind to do what ought not to be done (Rom. 1:28). In the future, those who allow themselves to be seduced by Satan (v. 9) will receive from God Himself this energy of error to actually believe in lies.

It is not that God will not have used patience and grace towards sinful man. Before the gathering of the believers to the Lord, He will have spoken through the prophets, His Son the Lord Jesus, and the Holy Spirit. Once again before the establishment of Christ's reign, He will offer salvation to everyone who receives the truth (Rev. 14:6). What more can He do if man deliberately rejects the truth?

in order that all may be condemned who did not believe the truth but had pleasure in unrighteousness. (2:12)

God's judgment is based on believing or not believing this truth of salvation in Jesus Christ alone. It is clear here that unrighteousness, which is even more characteristic of this future period than of the present time, will exert a greater attraction than truth. Moreover, those who are judged do not simply indulge in unrighteousness, but find their pleasure in it: the perversity of the heart of the unrepentant individuals is fully manifested. What a contrast with the work of

God who desires to accomplish in the believer all the good pleasure of His goodness (1:11)!

The false doctrine that the believers of the Church will suffer tribulations under the reign of the Beast and the Antichrist is gaining popularity today, and is likely to discourage many believers. However, as we have pointed out, a divine person, the Holy Spirit, and the presence of believers on earth are holding back the outbreak of an increasingly visible apostasy. As long as the Spirit and the Church are on the earth, the energy of evil will be held back. After their departure, the cry of distress of the faithful Jewish remnant will be heard during the great tribulation. The Church now says: Come, Lord Jesus! (Rev. 22:20). Not only does the Church foresee this day when she will meet Him, but also this other day when she will be manifested with the Beloved in glory before the world.

III

ENCOURAGEMENT FROM THE FATHER AND THE SON

Chapter 2, verse 13 to Chapter 3, verse 5

In these verses at the end of chapter 2 and the beginning of chapter 3, we will first be occupied with the results of the grace of God who has chosen us for salvation and the blessed prospect of obtaining the glory of the Lord Jesus. Understanding that God's salvation is a complete salvation will keep us from false thoughts such as believing that we must go through the great tribulation. Secondly, we will find that our responsibility is to hold fast the teachings of God's Word; it is through it that we will be encouraged by our Father and the Lord Jesus. Thirdly, we will be reminded that our prayers must include the servants of God who spread this good Word. We will conclude by mentioning the divine resources at our disposal to encourage us to obey God's Word.

a. *Results of God's Grace (2:13, 14)*

But we ought always to give thanks to God for you, brothers beloved by the Lord, because God chose you as the firstfruits to be saved [lit.: for salvation], through sanctification [or holiness] by the Spirit and belief in the truth. (2:13)

Those who will be judged and condemned will be the only ones responsible for their eternal punishment in the lake of fire. But thanks be to God, those who hear the Word and believe the One who sent Jesus have eternal life and do not come into judgment, but have passed from death to life (John 5:24). Do believers have any merit in this wonderful salvation? None, for it is God who chooses, who chose them in Christ before the foundation of the world (Eph. 1:4). We also make our own the words of the Lord to Israel: "I have loved you with an everlasting love; therefore I have continued my faithfulness to you" (Jeremiah 31:3).

God's salvation includes the salvation of our souls now (1 Pet. 1:9) and the salvation of our bodies at the time when the Lord comes for us and we are gathered together (1 Pet. 1:5; 1 Cor. 15:52). This salvation takes place in the sanctification, or setting apart, of the believer for God by the Holy Spirit, accompanied by faith in the Word of God. The Holy Spirit, together with the Word of God, does not operate only at the moment of conversion, but during the whole Christian life until we obtain the glory of the Lord.

To this he called you through our gospel, so that you may obtain the glory of our Lord Jesus Christ. (2:14)

God had entrusted Paul with the gospel as the means of calling the Thessalonians to salvation. We know that this gospel had come to them not only in word, but also in power and in the Holy Spirit, and with full conviction (or: in a great fullness of assurance) (1 Thes. 1:5). This good news had the future glory in view. Not just any glory, but the glory of our Lord Jesus Christ according to His own promise: "The glory that you have given me I have given to them" (John 17:22)—i.e., the glory received from His Father as Son of Man. As for His glory received as the Son of God, without sharing it, we shall see it (John 17:24). It is a happy prospect to think that we will soon be with our Beloved and that we will contemplate all His wonderful glories! Then we will cast our own crowns of glory before the throne and say: "Worthy are you, our Lord and our God, to receive glory and honor and power..." (Rev. 4:10, 11).

b. *Consolation and Strengthening (2:15-17)*

So then, brothers, stand firm and hold to the traditions [or instructions] that you were taught by us, either by our spoken word or by our letter. (2:15)

In his first letter, Paul had expressed the desire that his brothers and sisters should stand fast in the Lord (3:8). Despite the intensification of their persecutions and tribulations, his injunction is now to stand firm. One must not only resist the assaults of the enemies, but after overcoming everything, stand firm (Eph. 6:13). In times of respite, as well as in times of affliction, we must stand firm; the prospect of future glory will be a strong incentive to persevere in this regard.

The watchfulness of God's children will translate into an attachment to the teachings of God's Word. Such teachings are opposed to the teachings of men according to the elements of the world, not according to Christ (Col. 2:8, 22). It is incumbent upon us to keep the teachings of the Word as they have been given to us (1 Cor. 11:2). At the same time, the rejection of teachings that contradict or adulterate the Word of God will help us to stand firm in the midst of the ever-increasing apostasy.

Now may our Lord Jesus Christ himself, and God our Father, who loved us and gave us eternal comfort [*paraklēsis*: encouragement, consolation] and good hope through grace, (2:16)

What a source of encouragement to know that we are loved by the Lord Jesus and God the Father! Let us note the verbs in the singular in Greek: "who loved us and gave us..." In this love for us, the Father and the Son are one, just as Abraham and Isaac were one, and they went both of them together (Genesis 22:6, 8, 19). This encouragement, which has eternity in view, when we will be with the Lord Jesus

91

forever in the house of the Father, is given to us by the Father and the Son together. From the same source, we receive this good hope of seeing Christ manifested in glory and being at His side. God's grace is wonderfully unfolded to those who were once hateful and hopeless: who deserved to suffer an eternity away from God! What a precious motive for recognizing and praising God our Father and His Son the Lord Jesus Christ!

comfort your hearts and establish them in every good work and word. (2:17)

As in the previous verse, we note here a peculiarity in Greek grammar: despite the two subjects, the verb "comfort" is in the third person singular in the original Greek. We see here a testimony given by the Holy Spirit to the unity of the Father and the Son. The Son and the Father are one (John 10:30). These divine persons, from whom eternal consolation and good hope emanate, can also encourage our hearts and strengthen us in our daily walk. Sin produces so many sad circumstances that we would often be discouraged if we were not comforted by our Father and the Lord Jesus Christ. But we must look by faith, beyond earthly events, to these divine persons who are interested in us. We will then be strengthened to walk in the good works that God has prepared in advance (Eph. 2:10), and to speak that good word which will in turn rejoice the heart of another (Proverbs 12:25).

c. Paul and his friends' request for themselves (3:1-3)

Finally, brothers, pray for us, that the word of the Lord may speed ahead and be honored, as happened among you, (3:1).

Paul and his friends always prayed (1:11) and always gave thanks to God (1:3 and 2:13) for the church of the Thessalonians. These servants in turn sought prayers for themselves and their service. Although he was the object of special grace from the Lord as a chosen instrument for service (Acts 9:15), Paul remained humble and solicited the prayers of his younger brothers and sisters in Christ in Thessalonica. This twofold attitude suits us too: on the one hand, to seek the prayers of the saints for our various services for the Lord and, on the other hand, to pray for the servants of God.

Paul desired to see the word of the Lord whom he served spread rapidly. Isn't it our desire today to see this same Word speed ahead to save some and strengthen others? We give thanks to God for the freedom many countries enjoy and for the means at our disposal to spread the Word of God. But we must recognize that too often this Word is not glorified, because some people misrepresent it by behaving in a manner unworthy of the Master and thus bring it into disrepute. May the name of the Lord Jesus (1:12) and His Word be glorified, first of all, in our own lives, as they were among the Thessalonians despite their difficult circumstances.

and that we may be delivered from wicked and evil men. For not all have faith. (3:2)

The Thessalonians knew that glorifying the Word of God in their lives brought great tribulations. They had to face those men who did not please God and who opposed the preaching of the Word (1 Thes. 2: 15, 16). God wants all men to be saved, but many refuse to believe: they do not have faith. These men are wicked—literally in Greek: out of place—who therefore hinder the preaching of the Word, and evil because they oppose the work of God. Paul, more than any other, except the Lord Jesus, was familiar with the assaults of the Enemy. Only after he had asked his brothers for their prayers for the spreading of the Word, did he then ask for himself to be delivered from adversaries. In the evening of his life, he will testify that the Lord had rescued him from all his persecutions (2 Tim. 3:11).

But the Lord is faithful. He will establish you and guard you against the evil one. (3:3)

At the end of the first letter, Paul had reminded the Thessalonians of God's faithfulness (5:24). Here, our encouragement in the face of human opposition is also the Lord's faithfulness: He is with us, He does not leave us, and He does not forsake us (Joshua 1:5). As has been written, "His faithfulness responds to the faith of His people, however weak this faith may be". Moreover, the Lord strengthens us: He Himself being God, He is powerful to do this and He will do it until the end (Rom. 16:25; 1 Cor. 1:8). On earth, the Lord guards those who trust in Him against the evil one; at His side in heaven, between His coming for us and His coming with us, we will be kept from the hour of trial that will come on the whole world (Rev. 3:10).

d. *Divine resources (3:4, 5)*

And we have confidence in the Lord about you, that you are doing and will do the things that we command. (3:4)

Paul had in mind the welfare of these young believers; he desired to see Christ glorified in their Christian walk. His confidence that they would obey was not only based on what he knew of them, but it was also based on his trust in the Lord. It resulted from Paul's knowledge of the Lord's faithfulness to strengthen them and keep them from evil, as we have seen in the preceding verse. The Thessalonians had received the instructions (or commandments) of the apostle given through the Lord Jesus (1 Thes. 4:2): this was a further reason for the apostle to trust in the Lord that they would obey what He had commanded.

May the Lord direct your hearts to the love of God and to the steadfastness [or patience] of Christ. (3:5)

God's love and Christ's patience are divine resources to motivate us to obey God's Word. To obey is to respond to God's love manifested in His Son Himself. It is also to persevere in keeping His Word until Christ comes to seek His Church, at which time His patience will be rewarded. What lifts us above our circumstances and makes us children of obedience is not so much being occupied with our love for God and our patience while waiting to see the Lord. It is being occupied with God's love for us and Christ's patience as He waits to present the Church to Himself, holy and blameless (Eph. 5:24). Only the Lord can incline hearts to such things, just as He could effectively direct the way of Paul to them (1 Thes. 3:11).

It is always remarkable and a cause for rejoicing to see the extent of God's grace: it is manifested in time, but finds its source in eternity past (2 Tim. 1:9) and extends into eternity to come. Moreover, resources accompany this grace: we have pointed out the precious encouragement of the Father and the Son. Do not our hearts desire to be tuned to the love of God and the patience of Christ, already on this earth? May the Lord truly incline our hearts to such love and patience.

IV

ENCOURAGING AN ORDERLY WALK

Chapter 3, verses 6-15

From the privilege of being encouraged by God's love and Christ's mercy, Paul will now move on to practical exhortations about the Christian walk. Believers must not be overcome by their own circumstances: they must react and realize that they are responsible for walking in an orderly manner. Paul had been an example when he had been among the Thessalonians, so they knew how to imitate Paul and also how to behave towards the brothers walking in disorder. Paul addresses them directly with brotherly affection, but firmly. To walk in an orderly manner, as we shall see, is to do what is right in the eyes of God.

a. *Disorder in walking (3:6)*

Now we command you, brothers, in the name of our Lord Jesus Christ, that you keep away from any brother who is walking in idleness [or disorder] and not in accord with the tradition [or teaching] that you received from us. (3:6)

The Christian, who has the privilege of enjoying relationships with divine persons, must be conscious of his earthly responsibilities. As we saw in the first letter, he must judge everything that is contrary to holiness in his personal life (4:1-8). In this second letter, he is exhorted to keep himself pure by withdrawing from any brother walking in disorder: this is the exhortation or command of the apostle in the name of the Lord, the Head of the Church. Such a brother is like a soldier who will not keep in rank and who, by his behavior, could have a bad influence on the rest of the troop.

There is, however, a danger in summarily judging a brother without making an effort to win him back by the grace of the Lord. Matthew 18:15-17 is instructive in this regard. No effort should be spared to bring a brother back. Also, the law of the leper in Leviticus 14 shows us with what circumspection we should act in the Church of God in order to receive again a believer who has been under discipline. Every such disciplinary action, even if it has involved exclusion from the local church, must have restoration in view. The restoration of a disciplined believer is the fruit of God's grace. By showing love for the person from whom we had withdrawn (2 Cor. 2:8), but who is now restored, we are only confirming God's gracious work.

b. *Paul's walk (3:7-10)*

For you yourselves know how you ought to imitate us, because we were not idle [or: we have not lived in disorder] when we were with you, (3:7)

We must disassociate ourselves from a believer who is walking in disorder. Indeed, the collective reputation is affected by the individual walk of each brother and sister. If, as we read above, God's love and Christ's patience are precious resources for walking in order, we nevertheless remain responsible for our actions. Paul did not hesitate to offer the example of his own walk while he was among the Thessalonians. His conduct showed that he was imitating Christ (1 Cor. 11:1); they should all have looked up to such a model (Phil. 3:17).

nor did we eat anyone's bread without paying for it, but with toil and labor we worked night and day, that we might not be a burden to any of you. (3:8)

In his first letter (1 Thes. 2:9) Paul had made a similar remark. He could have lived from the gospel, as the Lord had commanded, but he preferred to make the gospel free of charge (1 Cor. 9: 14, 18). Paul worked with his hands making tents—this was his trade (Acts 18:3). It enabled him to provide for himself and for those who were with him (Acts 20:34). The Lord is glorified by servants who depend primarily on Him rather than on the bounty of brothers and sisters alone.

It was not because we do not have that right, but to give you in ourselves an example [or model, pattern] to imitate. (3:9)

As servants of the Lord, Paul and his companions deserved their food (Matt. 10:10). But more pressing interests had kept them from claiming this right in order to offer themselves as models to the young believers in Thessalonica. What an example the Spirit of God gives us with these words! Are we ready to act with conviction for the Lord, depriving ourselves of certain legitimate things, in order to offer ourselves as models for the benefit of the youngest? If not, to whom will they turn to?

For even when we were with you, we would give you this command: If anyone is not willing to work, let him not eat. (3:10)

If the servants of God worked hard and laboriously to be dependent on no one, how much more was it fitting for other brothers to work to earn their own bread? When he was among them, Paul had commanded them that he who was not willingly to work should not eat at the expense of others. Now in this letter he commands them to withdraw from any brother who was walking in idleness (or disorder) (3:6); a little further on he commands them to work quietly and to earn their own living (literally, in Greek: to eat their own bread) (3:12). Idle brothers seem to have used the coming of the Lord's day as a pretext to stop working. This reason was not valid since the gathering to the Lord, which is to precede the Lord's Day, had not yet taken place. Such behavior was unworthy of those who bore the name of Christ, and only created disorder.

b. *Exhortations to those who walk in disorder (3:11, 12)*

For we hear that some among you walk in idleness [or disorderly, out of rank], not busy at work, but busybodies. (3:11)

Only a few of the Thessalonians were walking in a disorderly manner, not working at all. But this was enough to dishonor the Lord and disrupt the life of the local church. Whether one is a Christian or not, idleness and the refusal to work encourage people to meddle in the affairs of others. For example, the idle Athenians and those who stayed in their city would spend their time in nothing else than exchanging news (Acts 17:21). This danger of idleness can also be a snare for young widows (1 Tim. 5:13)—and, of course, to all of us. A brother of our local church in the past, who is now with the Lord since many years, often reminded us of this verse: "Whatever your hand finds to do, do it with your might" (Ecclesiastes 9:10; see also Mark 14:7, 8). This brother was talking about the Lord's service, but we can also apply this verse to our secular work. We must not despise any work, however humble, whether it is for the Lord or to earn our own bread honestly.

Now such persons we command and encourage in the Lord Jesus Christ to do their work quietly and to earn their own living [literally, in Greek: to eat their own bread]. (3:12)

Paul and his friends use the verb *parakaleō*, to encourage, the tenth and last time in their two letters to the Thessalonians. They commanded and encouraged those who were walking in a disorderly manner to work quietly. They used both firmness and grace in addressing them in the Lord Jesus Christ, for it was a matter of the interests of the Lord and not merely a matter of acceptable social behavior. They were to be diligent and thus eat their own bread. Moreover, perturbed by the erroneous thought that the day of the Lord had come, their agitation was to give way to the serenity of waiting for the Lord's coming to take His people out of this world to Himself.

The lesson of this verse is salutary for each one of us who must provide for his or her own needs. Our circumstances at work may be difficult, even painful for some of us, but they should not result in worry and turmoil. Our resource is the peace of God which surpasses all understanding and guards our hearts and minds in Christ Jesus (Phil. 4:7).

b. *Exhortations as to those who walk in disorder (3:13-15)*

As for you, brothers, do not grow weary in doing good. (3:13)

This verse may also be read like this: "But you, brothers, do not grow weary doing what is right." It is less a question here of doing the good works that God has prepared beforehand, so that we may walk in them (Eph. 2:10), than of behaving according to the standards prescribed by God in His Word. The exhortation carries weight as we consider the influence that the walk of others may have on our own. The flesh within us can easily lead us to follow others in a path that will dishonor the Lord. We must be careful not to grow weary in doing what is right. Is there not a danger in wanting to do something else, however good it may be in our own eyes, without it being done in dependence on the Lord? In spite of the persecutions and tribulations, the Thessalonians, for their part, should not grow weary doing what was right.

If anyone does not obey what we say in this letter, take note of that person, and have nothing to do with him, that he may be ashamed. (3:14)

Disobedience to the apostolic commandments was a serious matter. One should not associate oneself with a brother who persists in a path of his own will, contrary to the word of the apostle in his letter. Such a brother was disobedient and, without going as far as excommunicating him, other believers should have nothing to do with him. The purpose of this discipline was to bring the brother, left to himself and to the Lord's work in his soul, to become aware of his condition, to repent, and to be restored to a better disposition.

Do not regard him as an enemy, but warn him as a brother. (3:15)

This brother, for whom Christ gave His life, but who does not obey His Word, must not be treated as an enemy. Both the warning and the affection of his brothers and sisters are together necessary and beneficial to him. In spite of the collective action of avoiding contact with him, this brother must feel the fraternal affection of his brothers and sisters who are waiting upon the Lord so that he may be regained and practical fellowship with him may be restored.

There are pitfalls when we are dealing with a brother or sister who walks in a way that dishonors the Lord. One mistake is to close our eyes and pretend that the Lord will take care of the person in trouble. To this attitude, we can object that our responsibility is to look after the interests of the Lord in a local church that claims to be His. Another attitude to be avoided consists in considering the guilty person as an enemy, e.g., to excommunicate this person purely and simply without having exhausted the resources of grace. This can only discourage this believer by creating distance from the church and sadly from Christ. Let us ask the Lord to give us wisdom to adopt proper conduct by showing grace and firmness in order to win back our brother or sister.

V

THE GREETING WITH PAUL'S OWN HAND

Chapter 3, verses 16-18

The last three verses of the epistle are the final salutation. Paul mentions the Lord three times: the Lord of peace, the Lord, and the grace of our Lord. The peace of the Lord was much needed by the Thessalonians in their persecutions and tribulations. His presence was with them at every step that brought them closer to the goal; He would support them to the end in a walk to the glory of God. The brothers and sisters could each avail themselves of the divine resources. His peace, presence, and grace are also assured to us as we wait to meet Him.

Now may the Lord of peace himself give you peace at all times in every way. The Lord be with you all. (3:16)

Only the Lord Jesus can give true peace to the soul of the one He has redeemed: "Peace I leave with you; my peace I give to you. Not as the world gives do I give to you" (John 14:27). If we cling to Him as faithful disciples, we will always experience this peace. Moreover, this same peace can be experienced regardless of our individual circumstances. Whether they were grieved over beloved ones who had fallen asleep in the Lord (1 Thes. 4:13) or overwhelmed by their own persecutions and trials (1 Thes. 1:6; 3:3; 2 Thes. 1:4, 6; see 2 Thes. 2:2), the Thessalonians could count on the peace of the Lord and on the Lord Himself. It was Paul's wish that all, both the anxious brothers concerned about the return of the Lord and the idle brothers, after having submitted to the Word, should experience the personal presence of the Lord to support and encourage them.

I, Paul, write this greeting with my own hand. This is the sign of genuineness in every letter of mine; it is the way I write. (3:17)

Paul had transmitted his teachings to the Thessalonians by word during his stay with them (Act. 17) and by letter (the two epistles written to the church of the Thessalonians). As we have seen, the brothers were to hold to these teachings (2:15). On the other hand, it seems that some had desired to worry the Thessalonians not only by word, but also by letter, even forging the apostle's signature. Paul must therefore warn them that writing greetings by his own hand is the means by which his readers are assured of the authenticity of his letters. It is noted elsewhere that Paul used the services of someone else to write a letter (Rom. 16:22), but wrote the final greeting with his own hand (1 Cor. 16:21; Col. 4:18). He had written the letter to the Galatians in full, but this was unusual (Gal. 6:11).

The grace of our Lord Jesus Christ be with you all. (3:18)

If the apostle wishes the Lord to be with them all, he also wishes His grace to be with them all. The grace of the Lord Jesus Christ is what gives every brother and sister the encouragement to persevere until He comes. In the first letter, the apostle's prayer was that this grace "be with you" (1 Thes. 5:28); here it is "be with you all." Whether they were brothers who might grow weary in doing good, troubled believers, or believers who were walking in disorder, all needed that grace.

This second letter must have comforted the young believers of Thessaloniki in their particularly difficult circumstances. Are our own circumstances sometimes difficult? The prospect of our gathering to our Lord Jesus Christ is meant to encourage us. This blessed hope also reminds us that the believers of the present time of grace will not experience the full manifestation of apostasy and suffering which will be the part of the faithful Jewish residue to whom the gospel of the kingdom will be entrusted (Matt. 24:14). While we wait to meet the Lord, we are called to walk in an orderly manner, working quietly for the glory of God and as a good example to those around us.

Our eternal encouragement will soon be to be with the Lord Jesus in the Father's house. May the encouragement of these two letters to the Thessalonians find an echo in our hearts as we wait to see and meet our Lord and Savior Jesus Christ!

GLOSSARY OF SOME TERMS

AFFLICTION 1 (*thlipsis*; from *thlibō*: to compress, to oppress) **Oppression, suffering.** This word is used re the disciples (Matt. 24:9), Joseph in Egypt (Acts 7:10), Paul (Col. 1:24), the Hebrews (Heb. 10:33), orphans and widows (Jas. 1:27). **2** (*mastix*) **Very distressing illness or evil.** This word is used re many who pressed on Jesus (Mark 3:10), a woman and others healed by Jesus (Mark 5:29, 34; Luke 7:21). **3** (to suffer affliction with: *sunkakoucheomai*; from *sun*: with, and *kakoucheō*: to mistreat, to torment) **To be mistreated with, to be persecuted with.** Moses chose to suffer affliction along with the people of God (Heb. 11:25).

CHOOSE 1 (*haireomai*: to take for oneself) **To decide, to select.** Paul did not know if he should choose to live or to die (Phil. 1:22). God had chosen the Thessalonians for salvation (2 Thes. 2:13). Moses chose to suffer affliction with God's people (Heb. 11:25). **2** (*hairetizō*; from *haireō*: to take) **To select.** Jesus was chosen by God (Matt. 12:18). **3** (*eklegō*; from *ek*: out, and *legō*: to choose) **To select, to elect; when God is choosing, it is His sovereign decision.** God will chose the elect during the great tribulation (Mark 13:20). Jesus chose twelve disciples (Luke 6:13; John 6:70; 13:18; 15:16, 19; Acts 1:2). Mary of Bethany had chosen the good part in listening to Jesus (Luke 10:42). Christians were chosen in Christ before the foundation of the world (Eph. 1:4). **4** (chosen: *eklektos*) **Selected, elected.** The Lord is a living stone chosen by God (1 Pet. 2:4). **5** (*epilegō*; from *epi*: upon, and *legō*: to say) **To express the choice, to select.** Paul had chosen

Silas to accompany him (Acts 15:40). Other ref.: John 5:2 (to call).
6 (*procheirizomai*; from *procheiros*: ready, at hand, which is from *pro*: before, and *cheir*: hand) **To select in advance.** God had chosen Paul to know His will (Acts 22:14). Other refs.: Acts 3:20; 26:16.
7 (to choose before: *procheirotoneō*; from *pro*: before, in advance, and *cheirotoneō*: to chose) **To select in advance.** The risen Christ appeared to witnesses chosen before by God (Acts 10:41).

CHURCH (*ekklēsia*; from *ekkaleō*: to call out) **a. The church (or assembly) of God is composed of all Christian believers redeemed by the blood of Christ, since the coming of the Holy Spirit at Pentecost until the return of the Lord.** Jesus is building His church (Matt. 16:18; see Eph. 2:20–22). The church is made of all the true believers in the Lord Jesus, known by God, who live at a certain time on earth (see 2 Tim. 2:19–21). Christ has loved the church and has given Himself for her (Eph. 5:25). Other refs.: Acts 2:47; 5:11; 8:1, 3; 1 Cor. 12:28. **b. The local church is made of all the true Christian believers living in a locality.** It is a gathering of Christians around the Lord in a given place (1 Cor. 11:16; 14:19, 34, 35). It is an expression of the universal church, the body of Christ (1 Cor. 1:2; 1 Thes. 1:1). Other refs.: Matt. 18:17; Acts 9:31. **c. Group of people gathered together.** The Greek term is used for the assembly of Israel in the desert (Acts 7:38). It also designates an assembly of citizens in Ephesus (Acts 19:32, 41) and a lawful assembly (v. 39).

COMFORT – See **ENCOURAGE**.

COMING 1 (*eleusis*; from *erchomai*: to come) **Arrival, advent.** This word is used re the first coming of the Lord (Acts 7:52). **2** (*parousia*; from *para*: beside, and *ousia*: pres. ptcp. of *eimi*, to be) **Presence; arrival, advent.** This word is used re the Lord Jesus (Matt. 24:3, 27, 37, 39; 1 Cor. 15:23; 1 Thes. 2:19; 3:13; 4:15; 5:23; 2 Thes. 2:1, 8; Jas. 5:7, 8; 2 Pet. 1:16; 3:4; 1 John 2:28), Stephanas, Fortunatus, and Achaicus (1 Cor. 16:17), Titus (2 Cor. 7:6, 7), Paul (Phil. 1:26), the antichrist

(2 Thes. 2:9), the day of God (2 Pet. 3:12). Other refs.: 2 Cor. 10:10; Phil. 2:12. **3** About the coming of the Lord Jesus, see **HOPE**.

CONSOLATION 1 (*paraklēsis*; from *parakaleō*: to comfort, to encourage, which is from *para*: near, and *kaleō*: to call) **Encouragement, exhortation; also transl.: comfort.** This word is used re the Holy Spirit (Acts 9:31), the Scriptures (Rom. 15:4), God (Rom. 15:5; 2 Cor. 1:3). God has given Christians an eternal consolation and good hope (2 Thes. 2:16), a strong consolation (Heb. 6:18). **2** (*paramuthion*; from *paramutheomai*: to comfort verbally) **Comfort, encouragement, solace.** Paul speaks of the consolation of love (Phil. 2:1). **3** See **EXHORTATION**.

DAY OF THE LORD (day: *hēmera*; Lord: *Kurios*; from *kuros*: supremacy) **Future day of the Lord's dominion on earth.** The day of the Lord will come as a thief in the night (1 Thes. 5:2; 2 Thes. 2:2; 2 Pet. 3:10, 12). There are other expressions equivalent to the day of the Lord (Acts 2:20): the day of Christ (Phil. 1:10; 2:16), the day of Jesus Christ (Phil. 1:6), the day of the Lord Jesus (1 Cor. 5:5; 2 Cor. 1:14), the day of the Lord Jesus Christ (1 Cor. 1:8), the days of the Son of Man (Luke 17:22, 26), the day of God the Almighty (Rev. 16:14), the day (2 Pet. 1:19).

ELECTION (*eklogē*; from *ek*: from, and *legō*: to choose) **Free and sovereign choice of God; also transl.: choice.** This word is used re Paul (Acts 9:15), Jacob (Rom. 9:11), a remnant among the Jews (Rom. 11:5), Israel (Rom. 11:7, 28), the Thessalonians (1 Thes. 1:4), Christians (2 Pet. 1:10).

ENCOURAGE 1 (*parakaleō*; from *para*: besides, and *kaleō*: to call) **To inspire and stimulate with courage to face difficulties, to console, to exhort; also transl.: to comfort.** Paul was encouraged by God that he might be able to encourage others (2 Cor. 1:4); when he was encouraged, it was for the encouragement of the Corinthians (v. 6). This verb is used re the brother who had been under discipline (2 Cor.

2:7), Paul (2 Cor. 7:6, 13; 1 Thes. 3:7), the Corinthians (2 Cor. 13:11), the Christians in Ephesus (Eph. 6:22) and in Colossae (Col. 4:8), the hearts of the Christians in Colossae, Laodicea, and elsewhere (Col. 2:2), the Thessalonians (1 Thes. 3:2; 4:18), the hearts of the Christians in Thessalonica (2 Thes. 2:17). Other refs.: Matt. 2:18; 5:4; Luke 16:25; Acts 20:12. **2** (to be encouraged together: *sumparakaleō*; from *sun*: together, and *parakaleō*: to encourage) **To encourage together by stimulating and inspiring one another to face difficulties, to console together.** Paul and the Christians in Rome would be encouraged mutually (Rom. 1:12). **3** (encouraged: *euthumos*; from *eu*: well, and *thumos*: spirit, passion) **Confident, cheerful.** The passengers on Paul's boat were encouraged (Acts 27:36). Other ref.: Acts 24:10 (cheerfully). **4** (to be encouraged: *eupsucheō*; from *eu*: well, and *psuchē*: soul) **To be comforted, to be more cheerful.** Paul was encouraged when he knew the state of the Philippians (Phil. 2:19). **5** (*protrepō*; from *pro*: toward, and *trepō*: to turn) **To urge morally, to inspire positively to do something.** The brothers encouraged Apollos (Acts 18:27).

ENCOURAGEMENT – See **ENCOURAGE, EXHORTATION.**

EXHORT 1 (*paraineō*; from *para*: by the side, and *aineō*: to prescribe, to praise) **To warn, to advise.** Paul exhorted the sailors to be of good courage (Acts 27:22). Other refs.: Luke 3:18 in some mss.; Acts 27:9. **2** (*parakaleō*; from *para*: beside, and *kaleō*: to call) **To encourage, to urge, to comfort.** This verb is used re the people, by John the Baptist (Luke 3:18), Peter (Acts 2:40; 1 Pet. 2:11; 5:1, 12), Barnabas (Acts 11:23), Paul and Barnabas (Acts 14:22), Paul and Silas (Acts 16:40), Judas and Silas (Acts 15:32), Paul alone (Acts 20:2; 27:33, 34), Jude (Jude 3). Paul uses the verb frequently in his epistles (e.g., Rom. 12:8; 1 Cor. 1:10; 2 Cor. 2:8; Eph. 4:1; 1 Thes. 2:11; 4:1, 10; 5:14; 2 Thes. 3:12). **3** (*protrepō*; from *pro*: toward, and *trepō*: to turn) **To urge morally, to encourage.** The disciples of Achaia were exhorted to receive Apollos (Acts 18:27). **4** See **ENCOURAGE.**

EXHORTATION 1 (*paraklēsis*; from *parakaleō*: to exhort) **Earnest advice or caution, encouragement, consolation; also transl.: appeal.** Paul and his companions were invited to give a word of exhortation to the people (Acts 13:15). He who exhorts should occupy himself in it (Rom. 12:8). He who prophesies speaks to men in exhortation (1 Cor. 14:3). Titus had received Paul's exhortation to go to the Corinthians (2 Cor. 8:17). Paul's exhortation was not of deceit, nor of uncleanness (1 Thes. 2:3). Timothy was to give himself to exhortation (1 Tim. 4:13). **2** (to exhort: *parakaleō*; from *para*: beside, and *kaleō*: to call) **Admonition, encouragement.** John the Baptist announced the glad tidings with many exhortations (Luke 3:18). **3** See **CONSOLATION**.

FAITH 1 (*pistis*; from *peithō*: to convince, to believe) **Trust, confidence; Heb. 11:1 says that faith is the assurance of things hoped for and the conviction of things not seen.** Faith comes by hearing, and hearing by the Word of God (Rom. 10:17). It is a gift of God (Eph. 2:8). Faith is presented in various aspects: **a.** the means by which one acquires salvation (e.g., Rom. 10:17; Eph. 2:8); **b.** the inner energy of the Christian fed by the Word of God and directed by the Holy Spirit (e.g., 1 Tim. 4:12); **c.** the whole range of Christian truths and divine blessings received by faith (e.g., Eph. 4:5); **d.** a particular gift of grace of use in the church (e.g., 1 Cor. 12:9). **2** (of little faith: *oligopistos*; from *oligos*: little, and *pistis*: conviction, faith) **Not believing or trusting very much.** The disciples were people of little faith (Matt. 6:30; 8:26; 16:8; Luke 12:28); Peter (Matt. 14:31).

GOSPEL 1 (*euangelion*; from *euangelos*: who brings a good news, which is from *eu*: well, and *angelos*: who brings news, messenger) **Good news, good message; also transl.: glad tidings. a. The Gospel of God's grace** (Acts 20:24) calls for faith in the person and work of Jesus Christ (see 1 Cor. 15:1–4). It brings salvation (Eph. 1:13) and peace (6:15) to sinners. **b. The Gospel of the kingdom** was preached by Jesus (Matt. 4:23; 9:35; Mark 1:14) and will be preached preceding His return to reign (Matt. 24:14; Mark 13:10; 16:15). **c. The**

everlasting Gospel (Rev. 14:6) proclaims the Creator God (see v. 7). **d. Other uses of the word Gospel:** of Jesus Christ, the Son of God (Mark 1:1), of God (Rom. 1:1), of His (God's) Son (v. 9), of Paul (2:16), of Christ (15: 19), of the glory of Christ (2 Cor. 4:4), to the uncircumcised (committed to Paul), to the circumcised (committed to Peter) (Gal. 2:7), of our Lord Jesus Christ (2 Thes. 1:8), of the glory of the blessed God (1 Tim. 1:11). **2 Name later given to each of the four accounts of the life of Jesus Christ narrated in the N.T.** Each gospel presents a particular aspect of Christ's person: Matthew, the King of Israel; Mark, the humble and perfect Servant; Luke, the Son of Man; John, the Son of God.

GRACE 1 (*charis*; from *chairō*: to rejoice; the word *chara* (joy) is also derived from *chairō*) **Unmerited favor which God, in His love, extends to the sinner who repents.** Grace is an unmerited favor granted without expectation of return; it is the free expression of God's loving kindness to men, motivated only by His bounty and benevolence. Its direct antithesis is *erga*, works (Eph. 2:8, 9). Grace forgives the repentant sinner, producing joy and thankfulness. Grace introduces a new creation (2 Cor. 5:17). (After S. Zodhiates). It brings salvation to the sinner (Eph. 2:5, 8; Titus 2:11), justifying this individual (Rom. 3:24; Titus 3:7). It accompanies Christians on earth (1 Cor. 15:10; 2 Cor. 12:9). Grace and truth came (sing. in Greek) by Jesus Christ (John 1:17). A gift of grace (1 Pet. 4:10) is for God's service. "Grace be with you" is a frequent closing salutation in N.T. epistles (Col. 4:18; Heb. 13:25; et al.). **2** (*euprepeia*; from *euprepēs*: beautiful, decent, which is from *eu*: well, and *prepō*: to be suitable) **Beauty, noble appearance.** The grace of the flower has perished (Jas. 1:11).

GREAT TRIBULATION (*thlipsis megalē*; tribulation: *thlipsis*; from *thlibō*: to afflict; great: *megas*) **Great distress, severe trouble.** This future great tribulation will be unequaled (Matt. 24:21: great tribulation; Mark 13:19: tribulation). It will come on Jezebel and her paramours (Rev. 2:22). An innumerable crowd will come out of it (Rev. 7:14).

HOLINESS 1 (*hagiasmos*; from *hagiazō*: to sanctify, which is from *hagios*: holy, which is from *hagos*: religious respect, reverence toward God) **Sanctification, moral purity.** Holiness is associated with righteousness (Rom. 6:19) and fruit (v. 22). Christ Jesus is made holiness to Christians (1 Cor. 1:30). This word is used re the sanctification of Christians in chaste living (1 Thes. 4:3, 4), Christians being called to holiness by God (v. 7) and being chosen for salvation through sanctification by the Spirit (2 Thes. 2:13; 1 Pet. 1:2), Christian continuing in holiness (1 Tim. 2:15), believers pursuing holiness (Heb. 12:14). **2** (*hagiotēs*; from *hagios*: holy) **Separation from evil according to the character and the nature of God.** Christians are disciplined that they may share in the holiness of God (Heb. 12:10). **3** (*hagiōsunē*; from *hagios*: holy) **Setting apart, separation in moral purity.** The Holy Spirit is called the Spirit of holiness (Rom. 1:4). The hearts of believers should be established in holiness (1 Thes. 3:13). They should perfect it in the fear of God (2 Cor. 7:1). **4** (*hosiotēs*; from *hosios*: holy, sacred) **Godliness, obedience to God.** Israel served God in holiness (Luke 1:75). The new man is created in holiness (Eph. 4:24).

HOPE (noun) **1** (*elpis*; comp. *elpō*: to give hope, to believe) **Contrary to human hope which includes uncertainty, the Christian hope has been described as a happy and confident expectation.** This word is used re what is invisible and future (Rom. 8:24; see v. 25), God for the Christians (Acts 24:15; 1 Pet. 1:21), God being the God of hope (Rom. 15:13), Jesus Christ who is the Christian's hope (Col. 1:27; 1 Tim. 1:1; 1 John 3:3), Israel (Acts 23:6; 26:6, 7; 28:20), Abraham (Rom. 4:18). Before their conversion, Christians had no hope (Eph. 2:12); unbelievers have no hope (1 Thes. 4:13). Christians now have the hope of glory (Rom. 5:2; 2 Cor. 3:12), of righteousness (Gal. 5:5), of the calling of God (Eph. 1:18; 4:4), of the gospel (Col. 1:23), of salvation (1 Thes. 5:8), and of eternal life (Titus 1:2; 3:7). Our hope is good (2 Thes. 2:16) and living (1 Pet. 1:3). The blessed hope (Titus 2:13) is the coming of the Lord for His saints (see 1 Thes. 4:15–18). **2** (to have hope: *elpizō*; from *elpis*: hope, trust) **To have confidence,**

to trust. We have hope in Christ in this life and afterwards (1 Cor. 15:19).

HOPE (verb) **1** (*elpizō*; from *elpō*: to wait upon, or *elpis*: hope, trust) **To place one's trust, one's hope in someone, something.** Gentiles were to hope in the Lord (Matt. 12:21; Rom. 15:12). Jews trust in Moses (John 5:45). Love hopes all things (1 Cor. 13:7). This verb is used re Christians (Phil. 2:19, 23; 1 Tim. 3:14; 2 John 12; 3 John 14), faith which is the substance of things hoped for (Heb. 11:1). **2** (to hope in return: *apelpizō*; from *apo*: from, and *elpizō*: see **1**) **To expect in return, to wish for in return.** We should lend, hoping for nothing in return (Luke 6:35).

IDOL 1 (*eidōlon*; from *eidos*: appearance, what one sees) **Material representation of a false god for the purpose of religious worship; the false god itself.** Sacrifices were offered to idols (Acts 7:41; 1 Cor. 8:4, 7; 10:19). Gentile Christians were cautioned to abstain from things polluted by idols (Acts 15:20). The Jew in Rom. 2:22 abhors idols. Before conversion, the Corinthians were led away to mute idols (1 Cor. 12:2). There is no agreement between God's temple and idols (2 Cor. 6:16). The Thessalonians had turned to God from idols (1 Thes. 1:9). Men will not repent of worshiping idols (Rev. 9:20). The injunction to keep oneself from idols (i.e., anything that would displace worship due to God) still applies to Christians today (1 John 5:21). **2** (idol's temple: *eidōleion*; from *eidōlon*: see **1**) **Place of pagan religious worship.** Eating in an idol's temple can wound the conscience of a weak brother (1 Cor. 8:10). **3** (thing sacrificed to the idol, thing offered to idols: *eidōlothuton*; from *eidōlon*: see **1**, and *thuō*: to sacrifice) **Remains of victims sacrificed to idols (i.e., false gods).** Paul speaks of things sacrificed to idols (1 Cor. 8:1, 4, 7, 10). Balaam and Jezebel would induce the Lord's people to eat things sacrificed to idols (Rev. 2:14; 2:20). Other refs.: Acts 15:29; 21:25; 1 Cor. 10:19, 28 in some mss. **4** (full of idols: *kateidōlos*; from *kata*: intensive, and *eidōlon*: see **1**) **Filled with idols (i.e., false gods), given up to idolatry.** Athens was full of idols (Acts 17:16).

IMITATOR 1 (*mimētēs*; from *mimeomai*: to imitate, to follow) **Person who reproduces the behavior of another, who follows a model; also transl.: example, follower.** Christians are exhorted to be Paul's imitators (1 Cor. 4:16; 11:1), imitators of God (Eph. 5:1), imitators of those who inherit what has been promised (Heb. 6:12), and imitators of that which is good (1 Pet. 3:13); other mss. have *zēlōtēs*: zealous. The Thessalonians became imitators of Paul and his companions, as well as of the Lord (1 Thes. 1:6) and of the churches of God (2:14) **2** (imitator together: *summimētēs*; from *sun*: together, and *mimētēs*: imitator) **Imitator with another person.** Paul told the Philippians to be imitators together of himself (Phil. 3:17).

JOY 1 (*agalliasis*; from *agalliaō*: to rejoice greatly, which is from *agan*, and *hallomai*: to leap) **Exuberant joy, exultation; also transl.: elation, exultation, great joy, gladness.** John the Baptist leaped with joy in his mother's womb (Luke 1:44). The disciples received their food with gladness (Acts 2:46). God anointed Jesus with the oil of joy above His companions (Heb. 1:9). God is able to present Christians before His glorious presence faultless with exceeding joy (Jude 24). Other ref.: Luke 1:14. **2** (*euphrosunē*; from *eu*: well, and *phrēn*: mind) **Joyfulness, gladness.** David said that God would fill him with joy (Acts 2:28). God filled men's hearts with joy (Acts 14:17). **3** (*chara*; from *chairō*: to rejoice; the word *charis*, grace, is also derived from *chairō*) **Gladness, delight. 4** (*charis*; from *chairō*: to rejoice) **Gladness, thankfulness.** Paul had great joy in Philemon's love (Phm. 7). **5** (to leap for joy: *skirtaō*; comp. *skairō*: to leap) **To jump for joy.** Jesus' disciples were to leap for joy when they suffered at the hands of men (Luke 6:23). Other refs.: Luke 1:41, 44.

LORD 1 (*Kurios, kurios*; from *kuros*: might, supremacy) **a. Title of God and of the Lord Jesus as those who have authority.** This title is used re God (e.g., Matt. 1:20, 22, 24; Rev. 21:22). Jesus uses "the Lord your God" when responding to Satan, (Matt. 4:7, 10). Jesus is Lord of all (Acts 10:36). Anticipating His return, Christians say: Come, Lord Jesus! (Rev. 22:20). **b. Person who has authority over**

another, master, sir. The servant is not above his lord (Matt. 10:24; John 13:16); it is enough for the servant to be as his lord (Matt. 10:25). The term is used in parables (Matt. 18:25–27, 31, 32, 34; 21:30; 25:11; Luke 19:25). It designates Pilate (Matt. 27:63), Paul and Silas (Acts 16:30), Abraham (1 Pet. 3:6), and an elder (Rev. 7:14). The Lamb is Lord of lords (Rev. 17:14; 19:16). Other refs.: 1 Cor. 8:5; Gal. 4:1. **c. Sovereign, emperor.** Festus referred to Augustus as his lord (Acts 25:26). **2** (*Despotēs*) **Sovereign master, one possessing supreme authority.** The term is used in addressing God (Luke 2:29; Acts 4:24; Rev. 6:10). **3** (Lord's: *kuriakos*; from *kurios*: see 1) **Which belongs particularly to the Lord.** This word is used only re the Lord's supper (1 Cor. 11:20) and the Lord's day (Rev. 1:10).

LOVE (noun) **1** (*agapē*; from *agapaō*: to love) **Deep feeling of affection, of attachment toward another person.** In the N.T., used only re divine persons (e.g., John 15:9; Rom. 15:30; 1 John 2:15) and Christians (e.g., Phil. 1:9; 2 Thes. 1:3). Has its source in God, and is expressed only by God and by those born of God (e.g., John 15:13; 1 John 4:8, 16, 18). Other ref.: 1 Thes. 3:6 "charity". **2** (love of the brothers, brotherly love: *philadelphia*; from *philadelphos*: one who loves his brother, which is from *philos*: friend, and *adelphos*: brother) **Affection, friendship between the brothers and sisters in faith.** Mutual (Rom. 12:10). The Thessalonians needed no instruction from Paul about it (1 Thes. 4:9). It is to continue (Heb. 13:1). Unfeigned (1 Pet. 1:22); added to godliness (2 Pet. 1:7). **3** (love, love toward man, love to man: *philanthrōpia*; from *philos*: friend, and *anthrōpos*: human being) **Benevolence, feeling of goodness toward the human race.** Of God the Savior has been manifested (Titus 3:4). Other ref.: Acts 28:2 (kindness). **4** (love of money: *philarguria*; from *philos*: friend, and *arguros*: money) **Avarice, inordinate greed for money.** It is a root of every evil (1 Tim. 6:10).

LOVE (verb) **1** (*agapaō*) **To take a deep and caring interest in someone or something. It denotes a deliberate choice, originating in the will and disposition of the agent and it is expressed by**

action. God loves the human race in general (John 3:16); the Father loves the Son (v. 35), and those who love the Lord Jesus (14:21). A new command: to love one another, as Jesus has loved us (John 13:34). **2** (*phileō*; from *philos*: friend) **To have tenderness, affection; to love as a friend.** The Father loves the Son (John 5:20) and the believer in Jesus (16:27). Jesus loved Lazarus (John 11:36). The man who loves his life will lose it (12:25).

MODEL – See **PATTERN.**

PATTERN 1 (*tupos*; from *tuptō*: to strike, as when using a stamp) **Example to follow, model; also transl.: ensample, example.** This word is used re the tabernacle built by Moses (Acts 7:44; Heb. 8:5), Paul (Phil. 3:17; 2 Thes. 3:9), Christians of Thessalonica (1 Thes. 1:7), Timothy (1 Tim. 4:12), Titus (Titus 2:7), elders (1 Pet. 5:3). **2** (*hupotupōsis*; from *hupotupoō*: to draw a sketch, which is from *hupo*: under, and *tupos*: see **1**) **Model, example.** This word is used re sound words (2 Tim. 1:13). Other ref.: 1 Tim. 1:16. **3** (*hupogrammos*; from *hupo*: under, and *graphō*: to write) **Pattern, model to follow.** Christ left us an example that we may follow His steps (1 Pet. 2:21).

PEACE 1 (*eirēnē*) **Cordial relations between individuals, mutual harmony; absence of violence, tranquility.** God is the "God of peace" (Rom. 15:33; 16:20; 1 Cor. 14:33; 2 Cor. 13:11; Phil. 4:9; 1 Thes. 5:23; Heb. 13:20). Jesus is the "Lord of peace" (2 Thes. 3:16). The word is used in various salutations (e.g., Luke 24:36; Rom. 1:7; 1 Cor. 1:3; 2 Cor. 1:2). Christians have peace with God (Rom. 5:1); Christ is their peace (Eph. 2:14). It is an integral part of the fruit of the Spirit (Gal. 5:22; also: Rom. 8:6; 14:17; Eph. 4:3). God has called Christians to it (1 Cor. 7:15). When the Lord left His own, He left them peace; He gave them His peace (John 14:27); though they have tribulation in the world, they have peace in Jesus (16:33). They are to pursue the things that tend to peace (Rom. 14:19), pursue it with the Lord's own (2 Tim. 2:22) and with all men (Heb. 12:14), seek and pursue it (1 Pet. 3:11). The peace of God guards their hearts and thoughts in

Christ Jesus (Phil. 4:7). This word is used in the expr. "to go in peace", i.e., "without care or worry" (Mark 5:34; Luke 2:29; 7:50; 8:48; Acts 16:36; Jas. 2:16). **2** to be in, to be at, to have, to live at, to live in peace: *eirēneuō*; from *eirēnē*: see 1) **To enjoy cordial relations, mutual harmony among people.** Christ's own are enjoined to be in peace (2 Cor. 13:11), with one another (Mark 9:50; 1 Thes. 5:13) and with all men, if possible, as far as depends on them (Rom. 12:18). **3** (to make peace: *eirēnopoieō*; from *eirēnē*: see 1, and *poieō*: to make) **To procure reconciliation, to bring about harmony.** Christ made peace by the blood of His cross (Col. 1:20).

POWER 1 (*dunamis*; from *dunamai*: to be able) **Might, capability, strength.** This word is used re God (Matt. 22:29; Mark 12:24; Acts 8:10; Rom. 1:20; 9:17; 1 Cor. 2:4, 5; 6:14; 2 Cor. 4:7; 6:7; 13:4; Eph. 1:19; 3:7, 16, 20; 2 Tim. 1:8; 1 Pet. 1:5; Rev. 11:17; 15:8), the Lord during His life on earth (Mark 5:30; Luke 4:14, 36; 5:17; 6:19; 8:46; 9:1), the Lord in glory (Matt. 26:64; Luke 22:69; Rom. 1:4; 1 Cor. 1:24; 5:4; 2 Cor. 12:9; Phil. 3:10; Col. 1:29; Heb. 1:3; 2 Pet. 1:3, 16; Rev. 15:8), the Lord at His coming to establish His future kingdom and reign (Matt. 24:30; Mark 9:1; 13:26; 14:62; Luke 21:27; Rev. 12:10), the Holy Spirit (Luke 1:35; 24:49; Acts 1:8; 10:38; Rom. 15:13, 19), Satan (Luke 10:19; Rev. 13:2), Elijah (Luke 1:17), Stephen (Acts 6:8), the apostles (Acts 3:12; 4:7, 33), angels (2 Thes. 1:7; 2 Pet. 2:11), Babylon (Rev. 18:3), the glad tidings (Rom. 1:16; 1 Cor. 1:18; 1 Thes. 1:5), the kingdom of God (1 Cor. 4:20), sin (1 Cor. 15:56), piety (2 Tim. 3:5), signs and wonders (Rom. 15:19). Power is attributed in praise to God (Rev. 4:11; 7:12; 19:1) and to the Lamb (Rev. 5:12). **2** (*dunatos*; from *dunamai*: to be able) **See 1.** God making His power known (Rom. 9:22).

RAISE (to raise up, to rise, to arise: *egeirō*) **To make a deceased person return to life.** The Lord raised up the temple of His body (John 2:19, 20). Jesus' resurrection from among the dead is a fundamental Christian doctrine (1 Corinthians 15): if He is not risen, the Christians' faith is vain (v. 12–17); but now He is risen from among the dead (v. 20), for the Christians' justification (Rom. 4:25).

This verb is used re His resurrection while yet future (Matt. 16:21; 17:23; 26:32; 27:63; Mark 14:28; Luke 9:22), and when accomplished (Matt. 27:64; 28:6, 7; Mark 16:6, 14; Luke 24:6, 34; John 2:22; 21:14; Rom. 6:4, 9; 7:4; 8:34; 1 Cor. 15:4; 2 Cor. 5:15; 2 Tim. 2:8). God the Father raised Jesus, His Son, from among the dead (Acts 3:15; 4:10; 5:30; 10:40; 13:30, 37; Rom. 4:24; 8:11; 10:9; 1 Cor. 6:14; 2 Cor. 4:14; Gal. 1:1; Eph. 1:20; Col. 2:12; 1 Thes. 1:10; 1 Pet. 1:21). This verb is used re John the Baptist per Herod's supposition (Matt. 14:2; Mark 6:14, 16; Luke 9:7), Lazarus (John 12:1, 9, 17), Isaac per Abraham's faith in God's ability (Heb. 11:19). At Christ's return, God will raise Christians who have died (1 Cor. 15:52; 2 Cor. 4:14). God raises the dead (Acts 26:8; 2 Cor. 1:9). See also **RESURRECTION**.

RESURRECTION 1 (*anastasis*; from *anistēmi*: to stand up, which is from *ana*: again, and *histēmi*: to stand) **Return to life of a person who has died.** Jesus spoke about resurrection (Matt. 22:30, 31; Luke 14:14; 20:35, 36), especially that of life and that of judgment (John 5:29). Lazarus would rise again in the resurrection (John 11:24). Jesus Himself is the resurrection John 11:25). Sadducees denied the resurrection (Matt. 22:23, 28; Mark 12:18, 23; Luke 20:27, 33; Acts 23:8), as did some Corinthians (1 Cor. 15:12, 13). Hymenaeus and Philetus said it had already taken place (2 Tim. 2:18). Jesus' resurrection (Acts 1:22; 2:31; 4:33; 26:23; Rom. 6:5; Phil. 3:10; 1 Pet. 1:3; 3:21) is at the foundation of Christian faith. Apostles announced the resurrection from among the dead, i.e., of Christians at the Lord's coming (Acts 4:2; 17:18), and the resurrection of the dead (Acts 17:32; 23:6; 24:21; 1 Cor. 15:42; Heb. 6:2; 11:35). There will be a resurrection of the just and of the unjust (Acts 24:15; Rev. 20:5, 6; see Rev. 20:13). Resurrection came by man, i.e., Jesus Christ (1 Cor. 15:21). Jesus is marked out Son of God by the resurrection of the dead (Rom. 1:4). Other ref.: Luke 2:34. **2** (*egersis*; from *egeirō*: to wake up) **See defin. in 1.** After the resurrection of Jesus, risen saints appeared to many (Matt. 27:53). **3** (*exanastasis*; from *ek*: out, and *anastasis*: resurrection) **Return to life of an O.T. believer or a Christian who has died.** Paul sought to arrive at the resurrection from among the dead (Phil. 3:11).

RISE – See **RAISE.**

SALVATION 1 (*sōtēria*; from *sōtēr*: liberator, savior) **a. Eternal redemption of a sinful person, obtained by repentance and faith in the perfect sacrifice of Jesus Christ at the cross.** This salvation is: so great (Heb. 2:3), ascribed to God (Rev. 7:10). Jesus Christ alone procures salvation (Acts 4:12); believers obtain it through Him (1 Thes. 5:9). Christ is its author (Heb. 2:9, 10). God chose Christians from the beginning for it (2 Thes. 2:13). It is of the Jews (John 4:22; 1 Pet. 1:10); the Lord sprang from the Jews; Himself and Him salvation were offered to them (Luke 1:77; 19:9; Rom. 10:1), then to Gentiles (Acts 13:26, 47; 16:17; Rom. 11:11; 2 Tim. 2:10). Grace that brings salvation has appeared to all men (Titus 2:11 (*sōtērios* see 3); 2 Cor. 6:2). The gospel is the power of God to salvation (Eph. 1:13; Rom. 1:16); with the mouth confession is made to salvation (Rom. 10:10). The salvation of their souls (1 Pet. 1:9) is a present reality for Christians (Phil. 1:28; see 1 Cor. 1:18). Their future salvation, when bodies of Christians will be transformed, is ready to be revealed (1 Pet. 1:5); they will inherit salvation (Heb. 1:14); it is nearer than when they first believed (Rom. 13:11). Christ will appear for salvation to those who wait for Him (Heb. 9:28). Presently, Christian salvation is continual deliverance from the servitude of sin (Phil. 2:12; 1 Pet. 2:2 in some mss.). Sorrow according to God works repentance leading to salvation (2 Cor. 7:10). It may also designate temporal deliverance (Phil. 1:19). The hope of salvation as a helmet (1 Thes. 5:8); the day of salvation is now (2 Cor. 6:2). Paul's affliction was for the Corinthians' salvation (2 Cor. 1:6). God's Word is able to make a person wise to salvation (2 Tim. 3:15). The Lord's patience is salvation (2 Pet. 3:15). Jude mentions the common salvation (Jude 3). Better things are connected to salvation (Heb. 6:9). This word is used re victory over Satan and Babylon (Rev. 12:10; 19:1). **b. Deliverance, liberation.** Zacharias speaks of a horn of salvation in the house of David (Luke 1:69), that they should be saved (lit.: a salvation) from their enemies (v. 71). God would deliver Joseph's brothers (lit.: give them salvation) by Joseph (Acts 7:25). Other ref.: 1 Thes. 5:8; see 2. **2** (*sōtērion*; from *sōter*: savior, liberator) **See a. in** 1. Salvation is of God (Luke 2:30; 3:6). It is offered to Gentiles (Acts 28:28). Christians have an helmet of salvation (Eph. 6:17: *sōtērion*; 1 Thes. 5:8: *sōtēria*). **3** (that brings salvation: *sōtērios*; from *sōter*: savior, liberator) **Which saves; see a. in** 1. God's grace that brings salvation has appeared to all men (Titus 2:11).

THANK – See **THANKS (GIVE)**.

THANKS (GIVE) 1 (*anthomologeomai*; from *anti*: in turn, and *homologeō*: to acknowledge, which is from *homologos*: assenting, which is from *homos*: same, and *legō*: to say; lit.: to acknowledge in turn) **To respond in praise, to celebrate in praise with thanksgivings.** Anna gave thanks to the Lord (Luke 2:38). **2** (*eucharisteō*; from *eucharistos*: grateful, which is from *eu*: well, and *charizomai*: to give, which is from *charis*: grace, which is from *chairō*: to rejoice) **To express gratitude.** This verb is used re the Lord Jesus (Matt. 15:36; 26:27; Mark 8:6; 14:23; Luke 22:17, 19; John 6:11, 23; 11:41; 1 Cor. 11:24), a leper healed by Jesus (Luke 17:16), and a Pharisee (18:11). It is used by Paul in his epistles (Rom. 1:8, 21; 7:25; 14:6; 16:4; 1 Cor. 1:4, 14; 10:30; 14:17, 18; 2 Cor. 1:11; Eph. 1:16; 5:20; Phil. 1:3; Col. 1:3; 3:17; 1 Thes. 1:2; 2:13; 5:18; 2 Thes. 1:3; 2:13; Phm. 4).

THANKSGIVING (*eucharistia*; from *eucharistos*: thankful, which is from *eu*: well, and *charizomai*: to give freely, which is from *charis*: grace, which is from *chairō*: to rejoice) **Prayer of gratitude; also transl.: giving of thank.** Paul speaks of saying amen at someone's thanksgiving (1 Cor. 14:16). This word is used re God and His glory (2 Cor. 4:15; 9:11, 12; 1 Thes. 3:9; Rev. 4:9; 7:12). Thanksgiving is becoming for saints (Eph. 5:4). Thanksgiving may accompany prayers and supplications (Phil. 4:6; Col. 4:2) and the walk of faith (Col. 2:7). We should make thanksgivings for all men (1 Tim. 2:1), receive foods created by God with thanksgiving (4:3, 4). Other ref.: Acts 24:3.

TRIBULATION (*thlipsis*; from *thlibō*: to compress, to oppress) **Physical or moral trial provoking great suffering; also transl.: affliction, distress, hardship, persecution, suffering, trial, trouble.** Believers have tribulation in the world (John 16:33). We must enter the kingdom of God with much tribulation (Acts 14:22). Paul boasted in tribulations, knowing that tribulation produces perseverance (Rom. 5:3; 12:12; 2 Cor. 6:4). God comforted Paul in all his tribulation that he might be able to comfort those who were in any tribulation (2 Cor. 1:4); Paul was exceeding joyful in all his tribulation (7:4). He did not want the Ephesians to not lose heart at his tribulations for them (Eph. 3:13). The Thessalonians received God's Word in much tribulation (1 Thes. 1:6). See **GREAT TRIBULATION**.

WRATH 1 (*orgē*) **a. Violent, intense anger as a settled disposition; also transl.: anger.** The law brings wrath (Rom. 4:15); Christians are to give a place for God's wrath (12:19); a ruler is God's minister to execute wrath on him who practices evil (13:4); Christians must be subject because of wrath (v. 5). Christians were children of wrath before their conversion (Eph. 2:3); all wrath is to be put away from them (4:31; Col. 3:8). Men are to pray everywhere, without wrath (1 Tim. 2:8). Christians should be slow to wrath (Jas. 1:19); man's wrath does not produce God's righteousness (v. 20). **b. Wrath of God.** This wrath expresses the horror that God has of evil. All unbelievers are under God's wrath; He will retribute evil (Matt. 3:7; Luke 3:7; 21:23; Rom. 2:8; 3:5; 9:22; Eph. 5:6; Col. 3:6; 1 Thes. 2:16; Heb. 4:3; Rev. 14:10; 16:19; 19:15). Jesus looked around with anger (lit.: wrath) at those in the synagogue (Mark 3:5). God's wrath abides on him who does not believe (or: obey) the Son (John 3:36). God's wrath is revealed vs. all ungodliness and unrighteousness (Rom. 1:18). The Lord is "slow to anger" (see Ex. 34:6), but once the day of grace will be ended, there will be the "day of wrath and revelation of the righteous judgment of God" (Rom. 2:5; Rev. 6:17). Jesus delivers Christians from the wrath to come (Rom. 5:9; 1 Thes. 1:10; 5:9). The Lord swore in His wrath against Israel (Heb. 3:11). Men will try to escape the wrath of the Lamb (Rev. 6:16): the day of the wrath to come (11:18). **2** (*thumos*; from *thuō*: to move impetuously) **Sudden burst of indignation, burning furor; also transl.: anger, rage.** All in the synagogue were filled with wrath vs. Jesus (Luke 4:28). Incited by Demetrius, Ephesians were full of wrath (Acts 19:28). Wraths should not be found among Christians (2 Cor. 12:20); wrath is a work of the flesh (Gal. 5:20). All wrath must be put away from Christians (Eph. 4:31; Col. 3:8). Moses did not fear the king's wrath (Heb. 11:27). God's wrath will be manifested vs. the inhabitants of the earth (Rev. 14:19; 15:1, 7; 16:1). **3** (*parorgismos*; from *parorgizō*: to provoke to wrath, which is from *para*: beside (intens.), and *orgē*: anger, wrath) **Exasperation, irritation.** The believer is not to let the sun set on His wrath (Eph. 4:26).

BIBLIOGRAPHY

Darby, J.N., *Études sur la Parole*. Éditions Bibles et Traités Chrétiens, Vevey, Suisse.

Hole, F.B. *2 Thessalonians*, in *Paul's Epistles* (Vol. 2), Central Bible Hammond Trust Limited, Wooler, England.

Horisberger, Marc. 1ère épître aux Thessaloniciens, in « *Sondez les Écritures* ». Bibles et Publications Chrétiennes, Valence (France).

Kelly, W. *Méditations sur les Épîtres aux Thessaloniciens*. Éditions Bibles et Traités Chrétiens, Vevey, Suisse, 1980.

Koechlin, Jean. *Chaque jour les Écritures*. Bibles et Publications Chrétiennes, Valence (France).

Pigeon, E. Richard. *Comprehensive Dictionary of New Testament Words*. AMG Publishers, Chattanooga (Tennessee), USA, 2014.

Pigeon, E. Richard. *Dictionnaire du Nouveau Testament*. Bibles et Publications Chrétiennes, Valence (France), 2008.

Pigeon, E. Richard. *Le due lettere di Paolo ai Tessalonicesi – Commentario*. Il Messaggero Cristiano, Valenza (AL), Italia, 2009.

Pigeon, E. Richard. *Pequeño Diccionario de las Palabras del Nuevo Testamento*. AMG Publishers, Chattanooga (Tennessee), USA, 2015.

Pigeon, E. Richard. Première Épître aux Thessaloniciens –
Commentaires sur une lettre d'encouragement. Bibles et Publications
Chrétiennes, Valence (France), 1987.

Pigeon, E. Richard. Seconde Épître aux Thessaloniciens –
Commentaires sur une seconde lettre d'encouragement. Bibles et
Publications Chrétiennes, Valence (France), 1988.

Remmers, Arend. Marc. 2e épître aux Thessaloniciens, dans « *Sondez
les Écritures* ». Bibles et Publications Chrétiennes, Valence (France).

Rossier, H. *Entretiens sur les Première et Deuxième Épîtres aux
Thessaloniciens*. Éditions Bibles et Traités Chrétiens, Vevey, Suisse,
1980.

The Holy Bible, English Standard Version. Crossway, Wheaton,
Illinois,USA.

Vine, W.E. *Expository Dictionary of New Testament Words*.
MacDonald Publishing Company, McLean, Virginia, USA.